SCHOLASTIC

studySMART™

Comprehension Skills

Level 3
English

For information regarding permission, write to:
Scholastic Education International (Singapore) Pte Ltd
81 Ubi Avenue 4, #02-28 UB.ONE, Singapore 408830
Email: education@scholastic.com.sg

For sales enquiries write to:

Latin America, Caribbean, Europe (except UK), Middle East and Africa
Scholastic International
557 Broadway, New York, NY 10012, USA
Email: intlschool@scholastic.com

Philippines
Scholastic Philippines
Penthouse 1, Prestige Tower, F. Ortigas Jr. Road,
Ortigas Center, Pasig City 1605
Email: educteam@scholastic.com.ph

Asia (excluding India and Philippines)
Scholastic Asia
Plaza First Nationwide, 161, Jalan Tun H S Lee,
50000 Kuala Lumpur, Wilayah Persekutuan Kuala Lumpur, Malaysia
Email: international@scholastic.com

Rest of the World
Scholastic Education International (Singapore) Pte Ltd
81 Ubi Avenue 4 #02-28 UB.ONE Singapore 408830
Email: education@scholastic.com.sg

Australia
Scholastic Australia Pty Ltd
PO Box 579, Gosford, NSW 2250
Email: scholastic_education@scholastic.com.au

New Zealand
Scholastic New Zealand Ltd
Private Bag 94407, Botany, Auckland 2163
Email: orders@scholastic.co.nz

India
Scholastic India Pvt. Ltd.
A-27, Ground Floor, Bharti Sigma Centre,
Infocity-1, Sector 34, Gurgaon (Haryana) 122001, India
Email: education@scholastic.co.in

Visit our website: www.scholastic.com.sg

First edition 2013
Reprinted 2013, 2015, 2018, 2019

ISBN 978-981-07-3287-5

Welcome to studySMART !

Comprehension Skills provides opportunities for structured and repeated practice of specific reading skills at age-appropriate levels to help your child develop comprehension skills.

It is often a challenge to help a child develop the different types of reading skills, especially as he encounters an increasing variety of texts. The age-appropriate and engaging texts will encourage your child to read and sift out the important information essential to read specific kinds of texts. As your child progresses through the levels, he will encounter a greater variety of skills and texts while continuing to practice previously learnt skills at a more difficult level to ensure mastery.

Every section targets a specific reading skill and the repeated practice of the skill ensures your child masters the reading skill. There are extension activities that can be done for specific reading skills to encourage your child to delve even deeper into the texts.

How to use this book?

1. Introduce the target reading skill at the beginning of each section to your child.

2. Let your child complete the reading exercises.

3. Reinforce your child's learning with an extension activity at the end of each activity. These activities provide additional practice, and extend your child's learning of the particular reading skill.

Note: To avoid the awkward 'he or she' construction, the pronouns in this book will refer to the male gender.

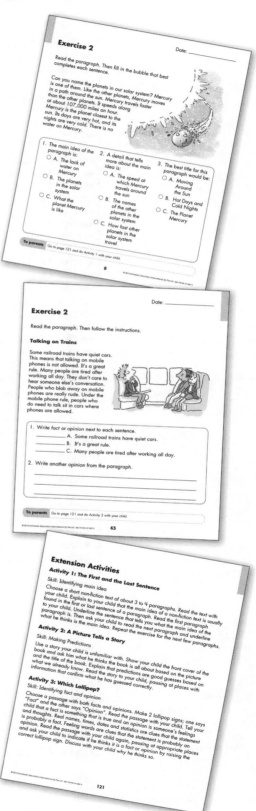

Contents

© 2013 Scholastic Education International (S) Pte Ltd ISBN 978-981-07-3287-5

Identifying Main Ideas and Details

Reading comprehension involves numerous thinking skills. Identifying main ideas and the details that support them is one such skill. A reader who is adept at identifying main ideas makes better sense of a text and increases his comprehension of what is being communicated. The passages and questions in this section will help your child learn to recognize main ideas and the details that develop them.

Understanding the main idea of a passage is to be able to have a broad overall understanding of what a passage is all about. This section will provide opportunities for your child to understand that supporting details fill in information about the main idea and that the main idea is bigger and broader than the supporting details.

The extension activities provide additional challenges to your child to encourage and develop his understanding of the particular comprehension skill.

© 2013 Scholastic Education International (S) Pte Ltd   ISBN 978-981-07-3287-5

Exercise 1

Read the paragraph. Then fill in the bubble that best completes each sentence.

Mum and Dad bought a jigsaw puzzle last Saturday. The jigsaw is a picture of an elephant spraying water on its back with its huge, long trunk. It is a majestic scene. There are two hundred pieces to the puzzle. I like doing the puzzle. Mum, Dad and I work on the jigsaw puzzle every evening after dinner. We are still working on it. We hope to finish it before next Sunday. We want to frame it up and give it to Grandpa for his seventieth birthday.

1. The main idea of the paragraph is:
   - ○ A. My birthday present
   - ○ B. An elephant spraying water
   - ● C. Doing a jigsaw puzzle

2. A detail that tells more about the main idea is:
   - ● A. Grandpa's birthday is on a Sunday.
   - ○ B. The cost of the jigsaw
   - ○ C. Mum, Dad and I work on the jigsaw puzzle every evening.

3. The best title for this paragraph would be:
   - ○ A. Grandpa's Birthday Present
   - ○ B. My Hobby
   - ● C. An Elephant Jigsaw Puzzle

To parents Go to page 121 and do Activity 1 with your child.

Exercise 2

Read the paragraph. Then fill in the bubble that best completes each sentence.

Can you name the planets in our solar system? Mercury is one of them. Like the other planets, Mercury moves in a path around the sun. Mercury travels faster than the other planets. It speeds along at about 107,000 miles an hour. Mercury is the planet closest to the sun. Its days are very hot, and its nights are very cold. There is no water on Mercury.

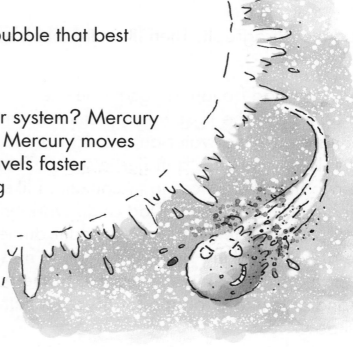

1. The main idea of the paragraph is:
   - ○ A. The lack of water on Mercury
   - ○ B. The planets in the solar system
   - ○ C. What the planet Mercury is like

2. A detail that tells more about the main idea is:
   - ○ A. The speed at which Mercury travels around the sun
   - ○ B. The names of the other planets in the solar system
   - ○ C. How fast other planets in the solar system travel

3. The best title for this paragraph would be:
   - ○ A. Moving Around the Sun
   - ○ B. Hot Days and Cold Nights
   - ○ C. The Planet Mercury

To parents   Go to page 121 and do Activity 1 with your child.

© 2013 Scholastic Education International (S) Pte Ltd ISBN 978-981-07-3287-5

Exercise 3

Read the paragraph. Then fill in the bubble that best completes each sentence.

Community names often have words for water in them. For example, Riverview is a town in Kansas. Running Springs is in California. You'll find Bay City in Michigan. Storm Lake is in Iowa, Great Falls is in Montana, and Brookfield is in Vermont. Where is Silver Creek? Why, it's in Mississippi.

1. The main idea of the paragraph is:
   - ○ A. Where to find Silver Creek
   - ○ B. Names of places with water words
   - ○ C. Different bodies of water in states

2. A detail that tells more about the main idea is:
   - ○ A. Which state has the most bodies of water
   - ○ B. In which state you'll find Bay City
   - ○ C. Why water words appear in names

3. The best title for this paragraph would be:
   - ○ A. Where Is Storm Lake?
   - ○ B. Water Words in Place Names
   - ○ C. How Communities Are Named

To parents   Go to page 121 and do Activity 1 with your child.

Exercise 4

Read the paragraph. Then fill in the bubble that best completes each sentence.

What foods cause the most problems in a car? Chocolate is one. It gets all over things. When drivers try to clean up the mess, they often have accidents. Hot drinks such as coffee are also dangerous. Why? They spill. Greasy foods cause trouble when they drip. Jelly doughnuts cause problems too. Can you guess why?

1. The main idea of the paragraph is:
   ○ A. Foods that are good for car rides
   ○ B. The problems caused by chocolate
   ○ C. Foods that cause problems in cars

2. A detail that tells more about the main idea is:
   ○ A. Greasy foods that drip cause problems.
   ○ B. Drivers should pay attention to the road.
   ○ C. Mobile phones are dangerous in cars.

3. The best title for this paragraph would be:
   ○ A. Chocolate Causes Accidents
   ○ B. Please Eat Neatly
   ○ C. Messy Foods in Cars

To parents Go to page 121 and do Activity 1 with your child.

© 2013 Scholastic Education International (S) Pte Ltd ISBN 978-981-07-3287-5

Exercise 5

Read the paragraph. Then fill in the bubble that best completes each sentence.

Beatrix Potter (1866 – 1943) loved animals. She also loved to draw. As a young girl, she kept a sketchbook of plants and family pets. She became a student of nature. Later on Beatrix Potter wrote stories for children. The main characters were animals. Perhaps you have read *The Tale of Peter Rabbit* or *The Tale of Squirrel Nutkin.*

1. The main idea of the paragraph is:
   - ○ A. Beatrix Potter's interest in nature
   - ○ B. The titles of Beatrix Potter's books
   - ○ C. The names of Potter family pets

2. A detail that tells more about the main idea is:
   - ○ A. How Beatrix Potter learned to draw
   - ○ B. What Potter drew in her sketchbook
   - ○ C. How the book *The Tale of Squirrel Nutkin* ends

3. The best title for this paragraph would be:
   - ○ A. Meet These Animal Characters
   - ○ B. The Words of Beatrix Potter
   - ○ C. Potter and the Natural World

To parents Go to page 121 and do Activity 1 with your child.

© 2013 Scholastic Education International (S) Pte Ltd ISBN 978-981-07-3287-5

Exercise 6

Read the paragraph. Then fill in the bubble that best completes each sentence.

Many U.S. presidents have had nicknames. James Madison was sometimes called Jemmy. Honest Abe was a popular name for Abraham Lincoln. Dwight Eisenhower was known as Ike, and Theodore Roosevelt was Teddy. Several presidents have been called by their initials. John F. Kennedy was JFK, while Lyndon B. Johnson was LBJ.

1. The main idea of the paragraph is:
   - ○ A. The nickname of President Eisenhower
   - ○ B. Nicknames for some U.S. presidents
   - ○ C. How presidents got their nicknames

2. A detail that tells more about the main idea is:
   - ○ A. Not all U.S. presidents have had nicknames
   - ○ B. Some nicknames have come from a president's initials.
   - ○ C. Only popular presidents have had nicknames.

3. The best title for this paragraph would be:
   - ○ A. Nicknames for Presidents
   - ○ B. Lincoln Was Honest Abe
   - ○ C. Who Was Jemmy?

To parents Go to page 121 and do Activity 1 with your child.

© 2013 Scholastic Education International (S) Pte Ltd ISBN 978-981-07-3287-5

Exercise 7

Read the paragraph. Then fill in the bubble that best completes each sentence.

Have you ever played Monopoly? This famous game was invented more than 70 years ago. Times were very hard then. Many people were out of work. Charles B. Darrow had lost his job too. He began designing games to earn money. One game was based on getting rich. For many people the game was a dream of better times. It became one of the world's most famous games.

1. The main idea of the paragraph is:
   - ○ A. How and why Monopoly began
   - ○ B. The reason Darrow lost his job
   - ○ C. How to play the game of Monopoly

2. A detail that tells more about the main idea is:
   - ○ A. What people liked about Monopoly
   - ○ B. How many people could play the game
   - ○ C. How much Monopoly costs

3. The best title for this paragraph would be:
   - ○ A. Meet Charles Darrow
   - ○ B. The Monopoly Story
   - ○ C. Popular Board Games

To parents   Go to page 121 and do Activity 1 with your child.

Exercise 8

Read the paragraph. Then fill in the bubble that best completes each sentence.

Do you know what a *chinook* is? It's a warm winter wind in the western United States. Another wind is a *purga*. This very cold wind brings snow to Russia. In France there is a dry wind called *mistral*. Egypt has a *khamsin*. This wind blows across the desert, stirring up sand. Around the world different winds come and go with the seasons.

1. The main idea of the paragraph is:
   - ○ A. Winds of the western U.S.
   - ○ B. How winds bring snow to Russia
   - ○ C. Different winds around the world

2. A detail that tells more about the main idea is:
   - ○ A. What a *purga* is and does
   - ○ B. Where the word *mistral* comes from
   - ○ C. How people dress during a *khamsin*

3. The best title for this paragraph would be:
   - ○ A. Cold Winter Winds
   - ○ B. What's the Weather?
   - ○ C. Winds of the World

To parents   Go to page 121 and do Activity 1 with your child.

Exercise 9

Read the paragraph. Then fill in the bubble that best completes each sentence.

Marc Brown writes books about an aardvark named Arthur. Many of Brown's characters are based on people in his life. For example, Buster is based on a childhood friend. So is the character, Sue Ellen. Two other characters, D.W. and Francine, are like his sisters in many ways. Another book character is Grandma Thora. She is named for Marc Brown's real grandmother.

1. The main idea of the paragraph is:
   - ○ A. How Marc Brown started writing the Arthur books
   - ○ B. Why Marc Brown's books have so many characters
   - ○ C. Where Marc Brown's characters come from

2. A detail that tells more about the main idea is:
   - ○ A. Who Francine is based on
   - ○ B. Why Arthur is an aardvark
   - ○ C. Where Marc Brown grew up

3. The best title for this paragraph would be:
   - ○ A. The Characters of Marc Brown
   - ○ B. Who Is Marc Brown?
   - ○ C. Meet the Real Grandma Thora

To parents Go to page 121 and do Activity 1 with your child.

Exercise 10

Read the paragraph. Then fill in the bubble that best completes each sentence.

An oyster lies on the warm sea floor. One day a speck of something gets inside the oyster shell. To protect itself, the oyster builds layers of a special material around the speck. The material is called nacre. After a few years a pearl is formed from the nacre. Someday a diver may find this natural pearl. It might become part of a valuable piece of jewelry.

1. The main idea of the paragraph is:
   - ○ A. How pearl divers work
   - ○ B. How a pearl is formed
   - ○ C. What the material nacre is

2. A detail that tells more about the main idea is:
   - ○ A. How natural pearls differ from cultured ones
   - ○ B. The names of the seas where natural pearls are found
   - ○ C. The role of nacre in forming a natural pearl

3. The best title for this paragraph would be:
   - ○ A. How Natural Pearls Are Made
   - ○ B. An Oyster's Life in the Sea
   - ○ C. Using Pearls in Fine Jewelry

To parents   Go to page 121 and do Activity 1 with your child.

Exercise 11

Read the paragraph. Then fill in the bubble that best completes each sentence.

Goats help prevent fires in California. In parts of the state, the fall season is very dry. Hot winds blow over the land. The smallest spark can start a fire. The fires spread easily through grasses and bushes. So people use goats to eat the plants as a form of fire control. The goats eat anything, even plants with thorns. Many people rent the goats until the rains come and the danger is over.

1. The main idea of the paragraph is:
   ○ A. Goats are not very fussy eaters.
   ○ B. Goats prevent fires by clearing land.
   ○ C. California's dangerous dry season

2. A detail that tells more about the main idea is:
   ○ A. The goats are rented for the dry season.
   ○ B. Cows do not work well for this job.
   ○ C. Goats also eat plants people want to keep.

3. The best title for this paragraph would be:
   ○ A. California Fire Safety
   ○ B. Goats as Firefighters
   ○ C. The Problems of Fall

To parents   Go to page 121 and do Activity 1 with your child.

Exercise 12

Read the paragraph. Then fill in the bubble that best completes each sentence.

People have used many materials to make maps. At first they drew on rocks, wood or clay. Sometimes they made maps on animal hides. Later mapmakers painted on silk or scratched on metal. On islands in the Pacific Ocean, people made sailing maps from sticks. The sticks were tied together to show the patterns of winds and waves. Tiny shells were added to show where islands were located.

1. The main idea of the paragraph is:
   ○ A. Using animal hides for early maps
   ○ B. Different materials used for maps
   ○ C. Sailing maps for the Pacific Ocean

2. A detail that tells more about the main idea is:
   ○ A. Using maps on the Internet
   ○ B. Maps were painted on silk
   ○ C. How the first globes were made

3. The best title for this paragraph would be:
   ○ A. Sailing With a Map
   ○ B. Sticks and Stones
   ○ C. Map Materials

To parents Go to page 121 and do Activity 1 with your child.

© 2013 Scholastic Education International (S) Pte Ltd ISBN 978-981-07-3287-5

Exercise 13

Read the paragraph. Then fill in the bubble that best completes each sentence.

On a summer night you might see the light of a firefly. This light is a mating message to other fireflies. Some ocean creatures also have lights. For example, the light on an angler fish helps it catch food. Other sea creatures with glow lights include jellyfish and shrimp. On land there are glow-in-the-dark creatures such as earthworms. Many kinds of animals have built-in lights.

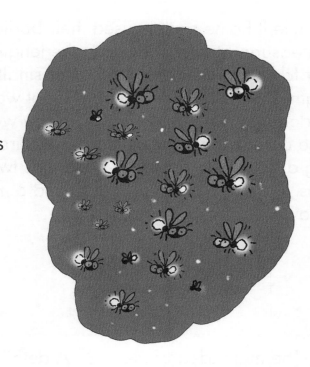

1. The main idea of the paragraph is:
   ○ A. The lights of summer nights
   ○ B. Creatures with built-in lights
   ○ C. Lights in the deep, dark sea

2. A detail that tells more about the main idea is:
   ○ A. How light helps an angler fish
   ○ B. The codes that fireflies use
   ○ C. How animals uses senses at night

3. The best title for this paragraph would be:
   ○ A. The Story of Light
   ○ B. Ocean Glow
   ○ C. Creatures of Light

To parents Go to page 121 and do Activity 1 with your child.

© 2013 Scholastic Education International (S) Pte Ltd ISBN 978-981-07-3287-5

Exercise 14

Read the paragraph. Then fill in the bubble that best completes each sentence.

In ancient Rome people used their bodies as measuring tools. They used the length of their foot to measure distance. For smaller lengths they used their thumb. A foot was divided into 12 thumb widths. Today we call these units inches. The Romans measured long distances in paces. A pace was two steps. A thousand paces was called a *mille*. Today we call this distance a mile.

1. The main idea of the paragraph is:
   - ○ A. Measurements of ancient Rome
   - ○ B. How inches were once measured
   - ○ C. Why Romans used feet to measure

2. A detail that tells more about the main idea is:
   - ○ A. How people once measured a yard
   - ○ B. How rulers were first developed
   - ○ C. How the Romans measured a mile

3. The best title for this paragraph would be:
   - ○ A. How We Got the Modern Mile
   - ○ B. Measuring from Head to Toe
   - ○ C. The Roman Way of Measuring

To parents Go to page 121 and do Activity 1 with your child.

Exercise 15

Read the paragraph. Then fill in the bubble that best completes each sentence.

People play chess all over the world. In a town in Italy people are the chess pieces. Every two years the town holds a human chess game. It is played on a huge chessboard painted in the town square. Some players such as the knights ride horses. All are in costumes to look like real chess pieces. Town officials call out the moves as large crowds of people cheer.

1. The main idea of the paragraph is:
   ○ A. Playing chess with people as pieces
   ○ B. A town square becomes a chessboard
   ○ C. How people play chess around the world

2. A detail that tells more about the main idea is:
   ○ A. How this human chess game got started
   ○ B. People who are knights are on horses
   ○ C. The history of the game of chess

3. The best title for this paragraph would be:
   ○ A. Human Chess Pieces
   ○ B. Costumes for Chess
   ○ C. Places to See in Italy

To parents Go to page 121 and do Activity 1 with your child.

© 2013 Scholastic Education International (S) Pte Ltd ISBN 978-981-07-3287-5

Exercise 16

Read the paragraph. Then fill in the bubble that best completes each sentence.

Most animals you see in cities are pets. You might also see some squirrels in city parks. But if you visit Thailand, watch out for monkeys. Many wild monkeys moved into the city of Lop Buri. There the monkeys are troublemakers. They go into houses and take things. On the street they snatch bags and eyeglasses. How do people get their things back? They give food to the monkeys.

1. The main idea of the paragraph is:
   - ○ A. Squirrels live in many city parks.
   - ○ B. Monkeys in Lop Buri steal eyeglasses.
   - ○ C. Wild monkeys cause trouble in Lop Buri.

2. A detail that tells more about the main idea is:
   - ○ A. Chipmunks are wild animals found in cities.
   - ○ B. The monkeys in Lop Buri enter people's homes.
   - ○ C. Thailand now has fewer forests than it once did.

3. The best title for this paragraph would be:
   - ○ A. Monkey Trouble
   - ○ B. Unusual City Pets
   - ○ C. The Food Exchange

To parents Go to page 121 and do Activity 1 with your child.

Exercise 17

Read the paragraph. Then fill in the bubble that best completes each sentence.

Pens have come a long way over time. The first pens were sticks with sharp points. Long-ago people used them to draw messages on wet clay. The ancient Egyptians made pens from hollow plant stems called reeds. They dipped the reed pens in paint or ink. Later, people used feathers called quills. Fountain pens were invented about 100 years ago. More recently, ballpoints were developed.

1. The main idea of the paragraph is:
   ○ A. How pens have developed over time
   ○ B. What kinds of pens were used long ago
   ○ C. The first pens

2. A detail that tells more about the main idea is:
   ○ A. Egyptians used reed pens.
   ○ B. Fountain pens were invented about 100 years ago.
   ○ C. Quill pens were made with feathers.

3. The best title for this paragraph would be:
   ○ A. Different Types of Pens
   ○ B. People Use Pens
   ○ C. How Pens Developed

To parents Go to page 121 and do Activity 1 with your child.

Exercise 18

Read the paragraph. Then fill in the bubble that best completes each sentence.

You have most likely seen pictures of log cabins. The story of log cabins begins with Swedish settlers in 1638. When the first Swedes landed in America, they built houses that were like those in Sweden. They fit together logs that had notched ends. They used clay or moss to fill in any spaces. Then they added a roof. These log houses were snug during cold winters and wet springs.

1. The main idea of the paragraph is:
   - ○ A. How log cabins are built
   - ○ B. History of log cabins
   - ○ C. History of Swedish Settlers in America

2. A detail that tells more about the main idea is:
   - ○ A. Swedish settlers went to America.
   - ○ B. Swedish settlers built houses similar to those in Sweden.
   - ○ C. There are many pictures of log cabins.

3. The best title for this paragraph would be:
   - ○ A. The Story of the Log Cabin
   - ○ B. History of Early Swedish Settlers
   - ○ C. Life in Early America

To parents   Go to page 121 and do Activity 1 with your child.

24   © 2013 Scholastic Education International (S) Pte Ltd   ISBN 978-981-07-3287-5

Exercise 19

Read the paragraph. Then fill in the bubble that best completes each sentence.

Birds make two kinds of sounds. They sing songs and they make call notes. Songs are used to attract a mate or to warn other birds off its territory. Call notes are used as a means of communication with other birds. They could also warn the birds of danger. For baby birds, call notes are used to let their parents know what they need. Sounds made by birds may sound the same to human ears. However, parent birds can always identify the cries of their own children.

1. The main idea of the paragraph is:
   - ○ A. How parent birds take care of baby birds
   - ○ B. Why birds make different types of sounds
   - ○ C. Why birds sing songs

2. A detail that tells more about the main idea is:
   - ○ A. Call notes are made to warn other birds.
   - ○ B. Birds sing songs when they are happy.
   - ○ C. Humans cannot hear as well as birds.

3. The best title for this paragraph would be:
   - ○ A. Taking Care of Baby Birds
   - ○ B. Sounds Made by Birds
   - ○ C. Songs Sung by Birds

To parents   Go to page 121 and do Activity 1 with your child.

Exercise 20

Read the paragraph. Then fill in the bubble that best completes each sentence.

Mother's Day is a special occasion celebrated by people all over the world. It is a day for children to express their love for their mothers. It is also an opportunity for children to thank their mothers for all their love and care. Children may treat their mothers to special meals, make or buy gifts, or do things to make their mothers feel special. Although people in different countries celebrate Mother's Day on different dates, the purpose behind this special day is the same.

1. The main idea of the paragraph is:
   - ○ A. Special festivals in the world
   - ○ B. When people celebrate Mother's Day
   - ○ C. Why and how people celebrate Mother's Day

2. A detail that tells more about the main idea is
   - ○ A. Children may treat their mothers to special meals.
   - ○ B. Children buy roses for their mothers.
   - ○ C. People celebrate Mother's Day in May.

3. The best title for this paragraph would be:
   - ○ A. Mother's Day
   - ○ B. Father's Day
   - ○ C. Love for Our Mothers

To parents Go to page 121 and do Activity 1 with your child.

Date: _____

Exercise 21

Read the paragraph. Then fill in the bubble that best completes each sentence.

Elizabeth Blackwell was the first woman to go to school to become a doctor. Elizabeth's friend once commented that she was sad because there were no women doctors to treat her. That prompted Elizabeth to become the first woman doctor. Elizabeth studied in Geneva College in New York. She graduated first in her class in 1849. She later opened a clinic for poor women and children. She also started a medical school for women who wanted to become doctors.

1. The main idea of the paragraph is:
   - ○ A. The life of Elizabeth Blackwell
   - ○ B. Medical school in Geneva College
   - ○ C. Helping the poor women and children

2. A detail that tells more about the main idea is:
   - ○ A. Many poor women and children could not afford medical treatment.
   - ○ B. What made Elizabeth decide to become the first woman doctor
   - ○ C. Why there were no women doctors in the 19th century

3. The best title for this paragraph would be:
   - ○ A. A Woman Doctor
   - ○ B. Importance of a Woman Doctor
   - ○ C. Elizabeth Blackwell

To parents   Go to page 121 and do Activity 1 with your child.

Date: _____

Exercise 22

Read the paragraph. Then fill in the bubble that best completes each sentence.

Oceans average about one cup of salt per gallon of water. Why are the oceans salty? Salt is a mineral found in rocks and soil. When it rains, water picks up salt from rocks and soil and carries it to rivers. Rivers then bring the salt with them when they flow into the oceans. The salt brought by the rivers accumulates over millions of years. Minerals from the ocean floor also dissolve and add to the salt content of the sea. These are the reasons why oceans are salty.

1. The main idea of the paragraph is:
   - ○ A. What forms the ocean
   - ○ B. Where can we find salt
   - ○ C. What makes oceans salty

2. A detail that tells more about the main idea is:
   - ○ A. Where salt in the ocean comes from
   - ○ B. Marine life in the ocean
   - ○ C. How we can get drinking water from the ocean

3. The best title for this paragraph would be:
   - ○ A. Where does Salt come from?
   - ○ B. The Story of the Ocean
   - ○ C. Salt in the Oceans

To parents   Go to page 121 and do Activity 1 with your child.

Exercise 23

Read the paragraph. Then fill in the bubble that best completes each sentence.

How do we know how much rain has fallen?
A meteorologist uses a rain gauge to measure the amount of rain that has fallen over a specific period of time. A rain gauge is a cylindrical like container left outdoors. When it rains, the rain gauge will be filled up with water. The meteorologist will then measure the amount of rainfall. Raindrops are smaller than we actually think. They are about 0.025 centimeters to 0.6 centimeters in diameter and they fall at a speed of between 3 and 8 meters per second in still air.

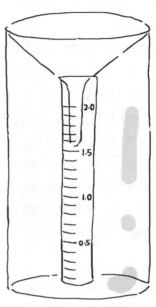

1. The main idea of the paragraph is:
   - A. How to measure rainfall
   - B. How big a raindrop is
   - C. How rain is formed

2. A detail that tells more about the main idea is:
   - A. Heavy rain could lead to a flood.
   - B. A rain gauge is left outside to measure rainfall.
   - C. Water droplets in the air form clouds.

3. The best title for this paragraph would be:
   - A. Measuring Rainfall
   - B. Measuring the Size of Raindrops
   - C. Formation of Rain

To parents Go to page 121 and do Activity 1 with your child.

Exercise 24

Read the paragraph. Then fill in the bubble that best completes each sentence.

Pop music started in the 1950s. When it first started, it was influenced mainly by rock and roll. Nowadays however, pop music is influenced by many styles of music. Pop music is music that appeals to a wide audience. It is also most often played on the radio. There are many famous pop hits and pop artistes, for example, Michael Jackson. He is often called the King of Pop.

1. The main idea of the paragraph is:
   - ○ A. Who Michael Jackson is
   - ○ B. What rock and roll is
   - ○ C. What pop music is

2. A detail that tells more about the main idea is:
   - ○ A. Pop music is fun to listen to.
   - ○ B. Pop music appeals to a wide range of people.
   - ○ C. Pop music is seldom played on the radio.

3. The best title for this paragraph would be:
   - ○ A. Pop Music
   - ○ B. Michael Jackson
   - ○ C. Different types of music

To parents Go to page 121 and do Activity 1 with your child.

© 2013 Scholastic Education International (S) Pte Ltd ISBN 978-981-07-3287-5

Making Predictions

Making predictions is one of the many essential reading skills that young readers need to have. A reader who can think ahead to determine what may happen next or how an event may turn out gains a richer understanding of a text. The passages and questions in this section will help your child learn to make reasonable predictions and anticipate probabilities.

This section will provide opportunities for your child to guess what is likely to happen based on information which he already knows as well as the information in the text.

The extension activities provide additional challenges to your child to encourage and develop his understanding of the particular comprehension skill.

© 2013 Scholastic Education International (S) Pte Ltd ISBN 978-981-07-3287-5

Exercise 1

Read each paragraph. Then fill in the bubble that best answers each question.

Cats' Feelings

Cats show their feelings in different ways. When they are happy, they purr and sit quietly. They may also roll over to get their tummy tickled. When they are angry, they hiss, growl and scratch. Their hairs stand on end and their tails twitch. Cats can also be playful.

1. Which sentence tells what most likely happens next?
   - ○ A. Cats will eat what you give them.
   - ○ B. Cats will leap, jump and chase anything available when they are in a playful mood.
   - ○ C. Cats will always dislike dogs.

A Frightening Experience

Molly loved watching her brother fish by the river when she was little. One day, while she was doing that, she tripped and fell into the river. The current was strong and Molly was swept away quickly. Molly's brother screamed for help as loudly as he could.

2. Which sentence tells what most likely happens next?
   - ○ A. A passerby will hear his cries and rescue Molly.
   - ○ B. Molly's brother will run away.
   - ○ C. Molly's brother will catch two big fish.

To parents Go to page 121 and do Activity 2 with your child.

Date: _____

Exercise 2

Read each paragraph. Then fill in the bubble that best answers each question.

Shapes and Edges of Leaves

Many leaves are round or oval. Others look like arrowheads, hands, feathers or hearts. Leaves also have different types of edges. In warmer climates, smooth-edged leaves are common. As moisture evaporates from leaves, the water rises through the roots. However, when it becomes colder, evaporation and water circulation stops.

1. Which sentence tells what most likely happens next?
   - ○ A. Plants will use leaves to make food.
   - ○ B. In cooler climates, there will be more tooth-edged leaves.
   - ○ C. There will be more leaves with chlorophyll.

Green Fingers

Terry went to Green Fingers with Mum and Dad last Sunday. Mrs Chan, the owner of the farm, gave them a packet of tomato seeds. Terry was thrilled to be able to plant his own tomatoes. The sun was strong and it was hard work tilling the soil.

2. Which sentence tells what most likely happens next?
   - ○ A. Terry will sell his tomatoes at the marketplace.
   - ○ B. Mum will suggest having tomato and cheese pizza for lunch.
   - ○ C. Terry will enjoy farming very much.

To parents Go to page 121 and do Activity 2 with your child.

© 2013 Scholastic Education International (S) Pte Ltd ISBN 978-981-07-3287-5

Exercise 3

Read each paragraph. Then fill in the bubble that best answers each question.

Birds' Feathers

Feathers are important to birds. They help identify birds by their varied colors and patterns, and they also keep birds warm. The fluffy feathers of birds trap warm air next to their skin. Feathers also help birds fly.

1. Which sentence tells what most likely happens next?
   - ○ A. Feathers will give wings and bodies a sleek, smooth shape.
   - ○ B. Feathers will be used as bookmarks.
   - ○ C. Feathers will be used in airplanes.

Christopher and His Mummy

Once there lived a tiny caterpillar called Christopher. One morning, Christopher woke up feeling very hungry. He started to look for Mummy for food. "Did you see my Mummy?" Christopher asked Little Worm. "What does your Mummy look like?" asked Little Worm. "Like me," answered a surprised Christopher.

2. Which sentence tells what most likely happens next?
   - ○ A. Christopher will make himself a cocoon.
   - ○ B. Mr Worm will laugh and tell Christopher that his mother looks nothing like him.
   - ○ C. Christopher will become a butterfly just like his Mummy.

To parents Go to page 121 and do Activity 2 with your child.

© 2013 Scholastic Education International (S) Pte Ltd   ISBN 978-981-07-3287-5

Exercise 4

Read each paragraph. Then fill in the bubble that best answers each question.

From Tree to Paper

How can trees be turned into paper? First, trees are chopped down and taken to paper mills. In the paper mills, the logs are grounded and mixed with water to make wood pulp. A machine then presses and rolls a layer of pulp into paper.

1. Which sentence tells what most likely happens next?
   - ○ A. Paper will be used in disposable cups and plates.
   - ○ B. Forests will diminish because many people chop down trees.
   - ○ C. The paper is dried and wound onto a large roll.

Ice cream

I love ice cream. It comes in different shapes, sizes and flavors. There is a flavor to suit everyone's taste. The most unique flavor is chewy bubblegum. However, my favorite is cookies and cream. Ice cream is the nicest thing to eat on a hot day such as today.

2. Which sentence tells what most likely happens next?
   - ○ A. Ice cream will make me feel happy.
   - ○ B. My sister will eat an ice cream.
   - ○ C. I will eat an ice cream.

To parents Go to page 121 and do Activity 2 with your child.

© 2013 Scholastic Education International (S) Pte Ltd ISBN 978-981-07-3287-5

Exercise 5

Read each paragraph. Then fill in the bubble that best answers each question.

Different Customs

People everywhere follow different customs. It is a good idea for travelers to know what these are in the places they visit. In China it is the custom to give special food to an honored guest. These include fish lips and fish eyes. Sometimes guests refuse such food.

1. Which sentence tells what most likely happens next?
   - ○ A. The Chinese will think their guests are rude.
   - ○ B. The guests will ask for the fish eye recipe.
   - ○ C. The Chinese will send out for pizza.

A Snowy Day

When Ellen wakes up on Saturday, there is snow on the ground. Ellen races through her breakfast. Then she pulls on a hat, jacket, and gloves. Her boots are not in the closet, so she runs outside in her sneakers. She joins her friends to go sledding.

2. Which sentence tells what most likely happens next?
   - ○ A. Ellen's feet will get cold and wet.
   - ○ B. Ellen will lose her sled on the hill.
   - ○ C. Ellen's friends will take off their boots.

To parents Go to page 121 and do Activity 2 with your child.

© 2013 Scholastic Education International (S) Pte Ltd ISBN 978-981-07-3287-5

Exercise 6

Read each paragraph. Then fill in the bubble that best answers each question.

Pompeii

Long ago, people lived in a Roman city called Pompeii, in Italy. Then a nearby volcano erupted. Pompeii was completely covered. Hundreds of years later, scientists began to dig it out. Little by little they have been uncovering the ancient city. They have set up museums to display the things they have found.

1. Which sentence tells what most likely happens next?
   - ○ A. The ancient people of Pompeii will come to life.
   - ○ B. Scientists will give up working at Pompeii.
   - ○ C. Scientists will continue learning about the past.

The Plane Contest

Jay and Chuck made paper airplanes. They decided to have a contest. Which plane could go the farthest? Jay went first. His plane glided well before it landed. Then Chuck sent up his plane. It didn't look as if it would go far. But suddenly a gust of wind came by. Chuck held his breath as his plane soared.

2. Which sentence tells what most likely happens next?
   - ○ A. Jay's plane will crash into a tree.
   - ○ B. Chuck's plane will go backward.
   - ○ C. Chuck will win the plane contest.

To parents   Go to page 121 and do Activity 2 with your child.

Exercise 7

Read each paragraph. Then fill in the bubble that best answers each question.

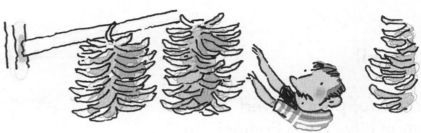

Paprika From Hungary

Hungary is known for its paprika. This red spice is used in cooking all over the world. Each Fall, the fields of Hungary are dotted with red plants. These are pepper plants. Once the peppers have been picked, they are hung on frames to dry. Then the dried peppers are ground into a fine powder. The peppers are now paprika.

1. Which sentence tells what most likely happens next?
   - ○ A. The paprika will be sold as a spice.
   - ○ B. The workers will all start to sneeze.
   - ○ C. The peppers will be sold for salads.

Bullet

Bullet is Barry's dog. Most days Bullet looks out the window at all the things he'd like to chase. When they go for a walk, Barry keeps Bullet on a leash. But today, while Barry was holding the door open for his Mum, Bullet slipped out.

2. Which sentence tells what most likely happens next?
   - ○ A. Bullet will wait for Barry to get his leash.
   - ○ B. Bullet will chase something in the yard.
   - ○ C. Barry's mother will praise Bullet.

To parents Go to page 121 and do Activity 2 with your child.

Exercise 8

Read each paragraph. Then fill in the bubble that best answers each question.

Taking Zoo Photos

Jessie is a photographer. Most of the time she works in a zoo. She loves her job, but it is not easy to get good pictures. The animals do not know they should stay still for a photo. So Jessie has to wait for just the right moment. Today Jessie is taking shots of the orangutans. They are her favorites. She knows they can be very silly!

1. Which sentence tells what most likely happens next?
   - ○ A. Jessie will yell at the orangutans.
   - ○ B. The orangutans will sit quietly.
   - ○ C. The orangutans will make funny faces.

The Rodeo

Steve went to the rodeo with his father. It was a very exciting day. Steve enjoyed the crowds, odors and sounds. He loved the animals and the colorful outfits of the riders. At school, Steve told his friends all about the rodeo.

2. Which sentence tells what most likely happens next?
   - ○ A. Steve will find out more about rodeos.
   - ○ B. Steve will forget all about rodeos.
   - ○ C. Steve's father will join the rodeo.

To parents Go to page 121 and do Activity 2 with your child.

Exercise 9

Read each paragraph. Then fill in the bubble that best answers each question.

Ladybugs

What do ladybugs eat? Their main food is a tiny insect called an aphid. Most gardeners think of aphids as pests. These insects cause harm to plants by sucking out their juices. When people see ladybugs in their gardens, however, they are pleased.

1. Which sentence tells what most likely happens next?
   - ○ A. Gardeners will get rid of the ladybugs.
   - ○ B. The ladybugs will eat the aphids.
   - ○ C. The aphids will attack the ladybugs.

Bill's Visit

Bill is an actor. He went to our school many years ago. Yesterday Bill came to visit the school. We were rehearsing a play. So Bill stayed to watch for a while. Later, he asked our teacher if he could talk to us.

2. Which sentence tells what most likely happens next?
   - ○ A. Bill will make fun of our play.
   - ○ B. Bill will offer some tips to us.
   - ○ C. Bill will ask to be in our play.

To parents   Go to page 121 and do Activity 2 with your child.

© 2013 Scholastic Education International (S) Pte Ltd   ISBN 978-981-07-3287-5

Exercise 10

Read each paragraph. Then fill in the bubble that best answers each question.

Space Junk

Did you know there is junk in space? This junk is made up of old satellites, rockets, and even tools lost by astronauts. Space junk can hit a spacecraft and damage it. Usually, scientists can guide a spacecraft away from space junk. But as more and more junk is left in space, the danger grows. So scientists are working on ideas for getting rid of space junk.

1. Which sentence tells what most likely happens next?
   - ○ A. Scientists will stop worrying about space junk.
   - ○ B. Space junk will start to fall to Earth.
   - ○ C. Scientists will find ways to clean up space.

Bert's Birthday

Sue knew that her brother Bert's birthday was coming soon. She wanted to buy him a gift. It was hard to decide what to get. One day Bert told Sue about a book he had read. It was about fish. Bert seemed really interested in this topic.

2. Which sentence tells what most likely happens next?
   - ○ A. Sue will serve fish for dinner on Bert's birthday.
   - ○ B. Sue will get Bert some goldfish for his birthday.
   - ○ C. Sue will forget to buy a present for Bert.

To parents   Go to page 121 and do Activity 2 with your child.

Exercise 11

Read each paragraph. Then fill in the bubble that best answers each question.

The Taj Mahal

The Taj Mahal, one of the world's most beautiful buildings, has a beautiful but sad story behind it. An Indian emperor, Shah Jahan, had a beautiful and intelligent wife by the title Mumtaz Mahal. Taj Mahal, the shortened form of Mumtaz Mahal means 'pride of the palace'. Mumtaz Mahal died in 1631.

1. Which sentence tells what most likely happens next?
   ○ A. Shah Jahan would build many famous monuments.
   ○ B. Shah Jahan would build the Taj Mahal in honor of Mumtaz Mahal.
   ○ C. Shah Jahan would change his title.

Paper Aeroplanes

Joseph likes to make all sorts of paper aeroplanes. He makes jet planes, cargo planes as well as helicopters out of different types of paper. One day, his teacher, Mrs Tabet, saw a poster about a competition organized by Yours Airline. Contestants are to create their own unique paper aeroplanes.

2. Which sentence tells what most likely happens next?
   ○ A. Joseph will train to become a pilot.
   ○ B. Joseph will build a real aeroplane.
   ○ C. Joseph will take part in the competition.

To parents   Go to page 121 and do Activity 2 with your child.

Exercise 12

Read each paragraph. Then fill in the bubble that best answers each question.

Spinning Tops

Spinning tops is a traditional game popular in the seventies. Since then, it has undergone some transformation. In the past, tops were made out of wood. A coil of string was wrapped tightly around it before it was flung onto the ground to make the top spin. Now a plastic rod is inserted into the top.

1. Which sentence tells what most likely happens next?
   - ○ A. Spinning tops will continue to be a popular game.
   - ○ B. People will only make tops out of wood.
   - ○ C. A pull of the plastic rod inserted into the top will make it spin readily.

Never Give Up

Patrick just fell again. He rubbed his badly scraped knees and wiped the perspiration off his face. He held onto the fence and pulled himself up again. "I must not give up. I must learn to rollerblade," Patrick muttered under his breath.

2. Which sentence tells what most likely happens next?
   - ○ A. Patrick will take a few more small steps.
   - ○ B. Patrick will sit on the ground and wail loudly.
   - ○ C. Patrick will give up and go for an ice cream instead.

To parents Go to page 121 and do Activity 2 with your child.

Exercise 13

Read each paragraph. Then fill in the bubble that best answers each question.

Making Waves

Waves are caused by wind blowing across the surface of the water. On a calm day, the wind blows gently and small waves swell across the water. On a stormy day, mighty winds create gigantic waves which crash onto the shore. Sometimes, a series of large water waves, called a tsunami, can occur.

1. Which sentence tells what most likely happens next?
   - ○ A. Many people will go surfing.
   - ○ B. The tsunami will cause a lot of damage.
   - ○ C. People will go swimming in the sea.

The Costume Competition

Stephen was extremely excited because his school was holding a costume competition on Friday. The students were to dress as their favorite fairy tale characters. For the past week, Mum and Stephen had been busy making costumes. Stephen wanted to be the Emperor from *The Emperor's New Clothes*.

2. Which sentence tells what most likely happens next?
   - ○ A. Stephen will watch a play.
   - ○ B. Stephen and his Mum will make a long, flowing red cape, a majestic crown and a scepter.
   - ○ C. Stephen will act in a play.

To parents Go to page 121 and do Activity 2 with your child.

© 2013 Scholastic Education International (S) Pte Ltd ISBN 978-981-07-3287-5

Exercise 14

Read each paragraph. Then fill in the bubble that best answers each question.

Journey by Railway Trains

Journey by trains can be very exciting. Trains travel on railway tracks which can continue for miles across the continents. Traveling by train is a cheaper alternative for travelers on a budget. It is also popular because travelers can enjoy the scenery as the train journeys across the various landscapes.

1. Which sentence tells what most likely happens next?
   - ○ A. Train travel will continue to be popular with travelers.
   - ○ B. The train is a safe mode of transportation.
   - ○ C. More people will take the plane.

Josephine's First Flight

"Pop! Pop!" go Josephine's ears. She felt more comfortable now that the pent up pressure had been released. She was not shocked because she had been warned about her ears. She was seated next to the window and looked out of the portholes.

2. Which sentence tells what most likely happens next?
   - ○ A. Josephine will feel hungry.
   - ○ B. Josephine will call for the air stewardess.
   - ○ C. Josephine will see lots of clouds in various shapes and sizes.

To parents Go to page 121 and do Activity 2 with your child.

Date: _____

Exercise 15

Read each paragraph. Then fill in the bubble that best answers each question.

Sharks

Sharks are fish. They live in oceans all around the world. They have large jaws and sharp teeth. They move very fast because of their streamlined shape. Sharks use their fins and tails to help them propel in the water. All sharks are carnivores.

1. Which sentence tells what most likely happens next?
   - ○ A. Shark will prey on fish or other sharks.
   - ○ B. People will hunt sharks for their fins.
   - ○ C. More people will know about sharks.

At the Beach

Last Sunday was a bright, sunny day. Jayme and Jayden were eager to go to their first outdoor painting class at Ma Wan Beach. They packed their art supplies, beach mat and water bottles. They also applied sunblock lotion and put on their caps and sunglasses. They met Max, their art teacher, at the beach.

2. Which sentence tells what most likely happens next?
   - ○ A. They will build sandcastles.
   - ○ B. They will meet some friends and swim at the beach.
   - ○ C. They will find a spot with a great view of the beach.

© 2013 Scholastic Education International (S) Pte Ltd ISBN 978-981-07-3287-5

Exercise 16

Read each paragraph. Then fill in the bubble that best answers each question.

The First Comic Book

A comic book is a collection of strips telling a single story or a series of different stories. Some of the comic books are reprints of popular strips in the newspapers. The first recognized comic book is *The Yellow Kid,* created by Richard Felton Outcault in 1895.

1. Which sentence tells what most likely happens next?
   - ○ A. Comic book writers will copy the drawings of prehistoric man.
   - ○ B. Comic books will be more popular with teenagers.
   - ○ C. Richard Felton Outcault would be the first person to use speech bubbles to tell what the characters say.

My Dad

Dad is a diligent man. He goes to work at eight every morning and comes home at half past seven in the evening. Although he must be exhausted, he always helps Mum get dinner ready for us. After dinner, he will look through my homework and read with me.

2. Which sentence tells what most likely happens next?
   - ○ A. Dad will change his job.
   - ○ B. If I don't have homework, Dad and I will have a game of chess.
   - ○ C. Dad will have a cup of hot chocolate before going to bed.

To parents Go to page 121 and do Activity 2 with your child.

Exercise 17

Read each paragraph. Then fill in the bubble that best answers each question.

Bees and Wasps

Bees and wasps are very different. A bee eats nectar gathered from flowers. A wasp eats ticks and flies. Bees live in a hive made of wax but wasps live in paper nests. A bee stings once and dies but a wasp can sting many times. Despite their differences, bees and wasps look quite similar.

1. Which sentence tells what most likely happens next?
   - ○ A. People will rear wasps for honey.
   - ○ B. People will often mistake wasps for bees.
   - ○ C. Wasps and bees will attack each other.

It's Fine to be Small

Samantha was small for her age. All the students in her class were taller and bigger than her. She was always the first in line and she couldn't reach the hook to hang her schoolbag. Fred, the class bully, called her "Teeny, Tiny Sam".

2. Which sentence tells what most likely happens next?
   - ○ A. Samantha will get sad when Fred teases her.
   - ○ B. Samantha will exercise rigorously, hoping to grow taller.
   - ○ C. Samantha will bully Fred back.

To parents Go to page 121 and do Activity 2 with your child.

© 2013 Scholastic Education International (S) Pte Ltd ISBN 978-981-07-3287-5

Exercise 18

Read each paragraph. Then fill in the bubble that best answers each question.

Rain or Shine?

Most people assume that umbrellas are invented for protection from the rain. We are not sure who invented the umbrella. However, we do know that in ancient times, the Chinese first used them as a form of sunshade. The umbrella was also a symbol of power and authority.

1. Which sentence tells what most likely happens next?
   - ○ A. Only royalty and those in the high office would use umbrellas.
   - ○ B. Raincoats would be invented for protection from the rain.
   - ○ C. Umbrellas would disappear during the Middle Ages.

Mud Fight

My brother and I love rainy days. We get ready for battle by putting on our dirtiest clothes and rubber boots. As soon as the rain stops, we dash out of the house. We make mighty canons out of mud and aim them at each other.

2. Which sentence tells what most likely happens next?
   - ○ A. Mum will not allow us into the house.
   - ○ B. We will fall in the mud.
   - ○ C. My brother will yell loudly when a ball of mud hits him.

To parents Go to page 121 and do Activity 2 with your child.

Exercise 19

Read each paragraph. Then fill in the bubble that best answers each question.

Stars

Stars are gigantic balls of burning gas that are scattered across the universe. They give off light and heat, and burn for millions of years. They die when they use up all their fuel and burn out. The hottest stars give off blue-white light.

1. Which sentence tells what most likely happens next?
   - ○ A. Stars will drop to earth when they die.
   - ○ B. The coolest stars will be red and dim.
   - ○ C. Stars will twinkle in the night sky.

The Inconsiderate Man

Linda was browsing through some books in the library when someone's mobile phone rang loudly. Everyone stopped reading and looked up. All eyes were on a man who started chatting on his phone. Though people around him stared at him, he ignored them and continued chatting loudly.

2. Which sentence tells what most likely happens next?
   - ○ A. The man's phone will run out of battery.
   - ○ B. The librarian will tell the man to turn off his mobile phone.
   - ○ C. Linda will go home.

To parents Go to page 121 and do Activity 2 with your child.

Exercise 20

Read each paragraph. Then fill in the bubble that best answers each question.

River Nile

The River Nile is the longest river in the world. It stretches across Egypt all the way to Sudan. In the past, traders bought and sold goods near or around the river as there was a steady supply of water for everyone. People soon began to settle around the river.

1. Which sentence tells what most likely happens next?
   ○ A. The River Nile will become a popular tourist spot.
   ○ B. Other countries will fight for the River Nile.
   ○ C. Cities will start to flourish along the River Nile.

The Adventures of Charlie and Alice

Charlie and Alice were at the fun fair with their parents. Alice and Dad had fun getting their photographs taken in silly poses. Dad was Spiderman scaling a tall building while Alice was Miss Muffet eating whey. Then, Charlie spotted the roller coaster.

2. Which sentence tells what most likely happens next?
   ○ A. Charlie and Alice will play for only two hours.
   ○ B. It will start to pour heavily.
   ○ C. Charlie will dash towards the roller coaster.

To parents Go to page 121 and do Activity 2 with your child.

Exercise 21

Read each paragraph. Then fill in the bubble that best answers each question.

Chickens

Chickens live in farms all over the world. They eat grass, seeds and worms. They get up at sunrise but sit on their nests all day long if they are hatching their eggs. Chickens have wings and can fly short distances. They fly up to roost on a safe perch at night.

1. Which sentence tells what most likely happens next?
   - ○ A. Chickens will fly away from their enemies.
   - ○ B. More chickens will live in the wild.
   - ○ C. *Chicken Run* will become a popular movie.

Harold, the Lucky Cat

Harold lives in the school. Mrs Evans, the head mistress, found him at the main gate when he was a kitten. Harold loves to rub against Mrs Evans' legs when she feeds him. He likes to curl up on her lap when she watches her favorite evening programs. Harold also loves the students in the school.

2. Which sentence tells what most likely happens next?
   - ○ A. The students will kick Harold.
   - ○ B. Harold runs around in the school.
   - ○ C. The students will play with Harold during their break.

To parents Go to page 121 and do Activity 2 with your child.

© 2013 Scholastic Education International (S) Pte Ltd ISBN 978-981-07-3287-5

Exercise 22

Read each paragraph. Then fill in the bubble that best answers each question.

Stick Insect

As its name implies, a stick insect looks like a stick. It is long, thin and brown. During the day, it hides by blending in with the branches and twigs of the tree. At night, it eats tree leaves. It can stay still for a long period of time.

1. Which sentence tells what most likely happens next?
   - ○ A. Birds looking for food will mistake the stick insect for a twig.
   - ○ B. Birds will find it easy to spot stick insects.
   - ○ C. The stick insect will fall asleep.

The Farmer and the Rabbit

On his way to the marketplace, a farmer saw a rabbit knock into a tree and die instantly. The farmer was overjoyed. He picked up the dead rabbit and had rabbit stew for dinner that night. The farmer thought, "It would be wonderful if I could have rabbit stew every night."

2. Which sentence tells what most likely happens next?
   - ○ A. The farmer will return to the same tree and wait for another rabbit to bump into the tree.
   - ○ B. The farmer will sell his vegetables at the marketplace the next day.
   - ○ C. The farmer will tell his wife to clean the house.

To parents   Go to page 121 and do Activity 2 with your child.

Exercise 23

Read each paragraph. Then fill in the bubble that best answers each question.

Heart Beat

The heart is a special organ. Unlike the muscles in our arms and legs, the heart does not have to be instructed to move. It beats on its own, almost like a car on auto gear. Automatic signals from the brain affect the rate the heart beats.

1. Which sentence tells what most likely happens next?
   - ○ A. The heart will weaken as we grow older.
   - ○ B. The heart will beat faster over time.
   - ○ C. The heart will continue to beat even if it receives no signal from the brain.

The Fox and the Stork

One day, a mean fox decided to play a prank on his friend, the stork. He invited the stork to his place for dinner. The fox served the stork some soup on a shallow dish. Try as he might, the poor stork could not have any of the soup because of his narrow bill.

2. Which sentence tells what most likely happens next?
   - ○ A. The stork will dislike the soup.
   - ○ B. The fox will gobble up his soup gleefully but the stork will still be hungry.
   - ○ C. The stork will thank the fox for a lovely dinner.

To parents Go to page 121 and do Activity 2 with your child.

© 2013 Scholastic Education International (S) Pte Ltd ISBN 978-981-07-3287-5

Exercise 24

Read each paragraph. Then fill in the bubble that best answers each question.

Flying South

Wild cranes fly south each fall. But cranes raised by people do not have parents to teach them how to do this. So scientists trained some cranes they had raised to follow a small plane. The pilot played a tape of adult cranes calling one another. Then the plane took off. The tame cranes followed it. The plane flew for two hours each day. So did the birds.

1. Which sentence tells what most likely happens next?
   - ○ A. The cranes will learn to fly south by themselves.
   - ○ B. The cranes will get into the plane with the pilot.
   - ○ C. Wild cranes will start to follow the plane too.

Marie's Candy

Marie had some chocolate candies. She ate one and gave one to her friend Judy. Then the girls decided to play jump rope. Marie left the candy in the sun while they played.

2. Which sentence tells what most likely happens next?
   - ○ A. The jump rope will get covered with chocolate.
   - ○ B. The girls will slip in the chocolate.
   - ○ C. The candies will melt in the sun.

To parents   Go to page 121 and do Activity 2 with your child.

Exercise 25

Date: _____

Read each paragraph. Then fill in the bubble that best answers each question.

A Special Museum

Have you read the picture book *The Very Hungry Caterpillar*? It is one of many books written and drawn by Eric Carle. In 2002 Mr Carle started a museum of picture books. The museum shows the art from different children's books. After looking at a picture, many children want to read the book it came from.

1. Which sentence tells what most likely happens next?
   - ○ A. The children will write a letter to the author asking for the book.
   - ○ B. The children will find the book they want in the library.
   - ○ C. The children will draw their own pictures on the museum wall.

After School

Clark was very hungry when he came home from school. His nose led him right to the kitchen. Something there smelled good! Sure enough, Clark saw his older sister taking some cupcakes out of the oven.

2. Which sentence tells what most likely happens next?
   - ○ A. Clark's sister will drop the cupcakes.
   - ○ B. Clark will ask his sister for a cupcake.
   - ○ C. Clark will do his homework in the kitchen.

To parents   Go to page 121 and do Activity 2 with your child.

56

Exercise 26

Read each paragraph. Then fill in the bubble that best answers each question.

The Loch Ness Monster

Loch Ness is a large lake in Scotland. Many people think a huge monster lives in the lake. The stories first started in the year 565. At that time reports said that a lake monster killed a swimmer. Since then many people have told tales about the monster. Some people have even made fake photos of it. Scientists have conducted tests but cannot prove it is real — or unreal.

1. Which sentence tells what most likely happens next?
   - ○ A. Loch Ness monster stories will continue.
   - ○ B. People will stop believing in the monster.
   - ○ C. The Loch Ness monster will come up on land.

Wildflowers

Holly went for a walk with her aunt and uncle. Along the way she picked some pretty wildflowers. Later they stopped to eat lunch on a rock by a stream. Holly was tired by the time they finally got home. The next day, she went to check on her wildflowers.

2. Which sentence tells what most likely happens next?
   - ○ A. Holly will find that her wildflowers have wilted.
   - ○ B. Holly will try to sell her wildflowers.
   - ○ C. Holly will plant the wildflowers in her garden.

To parents   Go to page 121 and do Activity 2 with your child.

© 2013 Scholastic Education International (S) Pte Ltd   ISBN 978-981-07-3287-5

Exercise 27

Read each paragraph. Then fill in the bubble that best answers each question.

Words, Words, Words

Will the word *muggles* soon appear in a dictionary? Words in the English language keep changing. Sometimes people stop using certain words. Very often new words enter the language. For example, *e-mail* came into use with computers. Dictionary writers keep busy tracking these changes.

1. Which sentence tells what most likely happens next?
   - ○ A. People will stop selling new dictionaries.
   - ○ B. The words in dictionaries will keep changing.
   - ○ C. The English language will run out of new words.

A Snowy Problem

It began to snow in the afternoon. Mr Burns watched it cover his yard and sidewalk. At about four o'clock the snow stopped. Mr Burns needed to go to the store. But the snow in front of his house was very deep.

2. Which sentence tells what most likely happens next?
   - ○ A. Mr Burns will shovel his sidewalk.
   - ○ B. Mr Burns will get out his sled.
   - ○ C. Mr Burns will wait for the snow to melt.

To parents   Go to page 121 and do Activity 2 with your child.

© 2013 Scholastic Education International (S) Pte Ltd ISBN 978-981-07-3287-5

Exercise 28

Read each paragraph. Then fill in the bubble that best answers each question.

Heat and Color

Dark things absorb, or take in, heat more than others. That is why dark clothes seem hotter in the sun. Dark, shiny cars feel hotter too. Light colors reflect the sun's heat away. In hot countries people often paint their homes white to keep them cooler. As warm summer months approach, many people change the clothes in their closets.

1. Which sentence tells what most likely happens next?
   - ○ A. People will start wearing light-colored clothes.
   - ○ B. People will start wearing dark-colored clothes.
   - ○ C. People will start painting their houses brown.

Doris Practices

Doris is a little short for her age. But she wants to play on the school basketball team. So Doris practises all the time. She plays with friends, her uncle, and her brother at home. Next week the coach is holding tryouts.

2. Which sentence tells what most likely happens next?
   - ○ A. Doris will decide to stay home.
   - ○ B. Doris will try out for the team.
   - ○ C. Doris will ask her brother to try out.

To parents Go to page 121 and do Activity 2 with your child.

Exercise 29

Read each paragraph. Then fill in the bubble that best completes each question.

Bird's Nest

Many Chinese believe that bird's nest soup is good for the health. They believe that bird's nest can make a person's body stronger. The nests of swiftlets are often harvested from caves in various Southeast Asian countries. They are then sold to many other countries. Bird's nest soup is expensive as it is quite rare. The harvesters continue to take more and more bird's nest every year.

1. Which sentence tells what most likely happens next?
   - ○ A. The number of swiftlets will decrease.
   - ○ B. Bird's nest will be made into other things.
   - ○ C. Countries will sell more bird's nest.

The Boy in the Jungle

Don went for a walk in the forest behind the old house. He was about to turn around and go home when he saw a strange sight. He saw a dirty looking boy talking to a monkey. The boy was wearing some fur around him and standing like a monkey. He looked strange but friendly.

2. Which sentence tells what most likely happens next?
   - ○ A. Don will run away.
   - ○ B. Don will start walking like a monkey as well.
   - ○ C. Don will try to talk to the boy.

To parents Go to page 121 and do Activity 2 with your child.

© 2013 Scholastic Education International (S) Pte Ltd ISBN 978-981-07-3287-5

Identifying Fact and Opinion

Being able to identify and distinguish between a fact and an opinion is an important reading comprehension skill, especially as readers start to encounter a variety of texts. A reader who can differentiate between statements of fact and opinion are better able to analyze and assess a text. The passages and questions in this section will help your child learn to identify statements of fact and opinion.

This section will provide opportunities for your child to understand that a fact can be proved to be true, while an opinion is what someone thinks or believes and is a kind of judgement.

The extension activities provide additional challenges to your child to encourage and develop his understanding of the particular comprehension skill.

© 2013 Scholastic Education International (S) Pte Ltd ISBN 978-981-07-3287-5

Exercise 1

Read the paragraph. Then follow the instructions.

Classroom Pets

Many classrooms have pets. This is
the best way for students to learn about
animals. But classroom pets need
a place to go during the summer.
In Plano, Texas, the schools have
a mini-zoo. Teachers can borrow pets
for the school months. When summer
comes, they return the pets to the zoo.
Schools in other towns should follow
this example.

1. Write *fact* or *opinion* next to each sentence.

   _____ A. This is the best way for students to learn about animals.

   _____ B. In Plano, Texas, the schools have a mini-zoo.

   _____ C. Schools in other towns should follow this example.

2. Write another fact from the paragraph.

   _____

   _____

   _____

To parents Go to page 121 and do Activity 3 with your child.

Exercise 2

Read the paragraph. Then follow the instructions.

Talking on Trains

Some railroad trains have quiet cars. This means that talking on mobile phones is not allowed. It's a great rule. Many people are tired after working all day. They don't care to hear someone else's conversation. People who blab away on mobile phones are really rude. Under the mobile phone rule, people who do need to talk sit in cars where phones are allowed.

1. Write *fact* or *opinion* next to each sentence.

    _____ A. Some railroad trains have quiet cars.

    _____ B. It's a great rule.

    _____ C. Many people are tired after working all day.

2. Write another opinion from the paragraph.

    _____

    _____

    _____

To parents Go to page 121 and do Activity 3 with your child.

Exercise 3

Read the paragraph. Then follow the instructions.

Nesting Dolls

Nesting dolls are sets of wooden dolls. I think they are very cute. You twist open each doll to find another, smaller doll inside. These dolls were first made in Russia in 1890. Today major league baseball teams are handing out these dolls. They are called Stackable Stars. Each doll is painted to look like a player on the team. Many fans collect the dolls.

1. Write *fact* or *opinion* next to each sentence.

   _____ A. I think they are very cute.

   _____ B. Today major league baseball teams are handing out these dolls.

   _____ C. Many fans collect the dolls.

2. Write another fact from the paragraph.

   _____

   _____

   _____

To parents Go to page 121 and do Activity 3 with your child.

64

Exercise 4

Read the paragraph. Then follow the instructions.

An Unusual Race

Many places have boat races. But the town of Rieti in Italy has a washtub race. What a silly event! The race takes place on the Velino River. The racers, all men, kneel in the tubs. They use oars to paddle. If a racer isn't careful, the tub tips over. Also, if a racer doesn't paddle correctly, the tub spins around. In my opinion, you have to be a good sport for this race.

1. Write *fact* or *opinion* next to each sentence.

   _____ A. The race takes place on the Velino River.

   _____ B. What a silly event!

   _____ C. The racers, all men, kneel in the tubs.

2. Write another opinion from the paragraph.

   _____

   _____

   _____

To parents   Go to page 121 and do Activity 3 with your child.

Exercise 5

Read the paragraph. Then follow the instructions.

White Rhinos

One of the most amazing sights at a zoo is the white rhino. This animal is quite rare. It is the largest of the five kinds of rhinos. Zookeepers report that white rhinos like spaces that are dry and dusty. They must be rather messy animals. In the wild, the white rhino is a target of hunters. They kill these rhinos for their horns. That's horrible!

1. Write *fact* or *opinion* next to each sentence.

   _____ A. It is the largest of the five kinds of rhinos.

   _____ B. One of the most amazing sights at a zoo is the white rhino.

   _____ C. That's horrible!

2. Write another opinion from the paragraph.

   _____

   _____

   _____

To parents   Go to page 121 and do Activity 3 with your child.

Exercise 6

Read the paragraph. Then follow the instructions.

Big Cat

The jaguar is one of the four big cats.
The others are lions, tigers and leopards.
Jaguars live in warm climates in Latin
America. They are the most beautiful of all
wild cats. A jaguar has a big head and a
strong jaw. Its paws and claws are huge.
The jaguar is a silent and deadly hunter.
However, it rarely attacks people. The
jaguar spends most of its time alone and
even stays away from other jaguars.

1. Write *fact* or *opinion* next to each sentence.

   _____ A. The jaguar is one of the four big cats.

   _____ B. Jaguars live in warm climates in Latin America.

   _____ C. They are the most beautiful of all wild cats.

2. Write another fact from the paragraph.

   _____

   _____

   _____

To parents   Go to page 121 and do Activity 3 with your child.

Exercise 7

Read the paragraph. Then follow the instructions.

Some Soup!

Birds called swifts are popular in Thailand.
People there welcome the birds into their
homes. In one city the birds even live in
a hotel. The reason the birds are in such
demand is their nests. Bird's nest soup is
a big treat in Thailand. I don't think
I would care for it. Vegetable soup seems
better to me!

1. Write *fact* or *opinion* next to each sentence.

   _____ A. Birds called swifts are popular in Thailand.

   _____ B. I don't think I would care for it.

   _____ C. In one city the birds even live in a hotel.

2. Write another opinion from the paragraph.

   _____

   _____

   _____

To parents Go to page 121 and do Activity 3 with your child.

Exercise 8

Read the paragraph. Then follow the instructions.

Family Fun Long Ago

People in ancient Egypt weren't lucky enough to have televisions or computers. They spent their free time in other ways. Families often went on outings along the Nile River. Sometimes they sailed in boats. Often the children caught fish with spears or nets. They also picked flowers that grew along the shores. Children today have a lot more fun.

1. Write *fact* or *opinion* next to each sentence.

   _____ A. Families often went on outings along the Nile River.

   _____ B. Children today have a lot more fun.

   _____ C. Often the children caught fish with spears or nets.

2. Write another fact from the paragraph.

   _____

   _____

   _____

To parents   Go to page 121 and do Activity 3 with your child.

Date: _____

Exercise 9

Read the paragraph. Then follow the instructions.

Where Chess Is Big

In North Carolina an artist makes huge chess sets. The sets take up most of a backyard. The pieces are made from "found" materials, usually metal. Each piece is fabulous! To play the game, people walk around on the board. When they are ready to move, they have to push or pull the pieces. This must be the most fun way to play chess.

1. Write *fact* or *opinion* next to each sentence.

    _____ A. In North Carolina an artist makes huge chess sets.

    _____ B. To play the game, people walk around on the board.

    _____ C. Each piece is fabulous!

2. Write another opinion from the paragraph.

    _____

    _____

    _____

To parents Go to page 121 and do Activity 3 with your child.

Exercise 10

Read the paragraph. Then follow the instructions.

Staying Warm

Everyone should learn about the
animals of the Arctic. These
animals are super. They have
special ways of living in the cold.
For example, the musk ox has two
layers of fur. The inner layer traps
air warmed by the animal's body.
The outer layer has long hairs
that protect the ox from wind and
water. What a great way to
stay warm!

1. Write *fact* or *opinion* next to each sentence.

_____ A. Everyone should learn about the animals of the Arctic.

_____ B. What a great way to stay warm!

_____ C. The inner layer traps air warmed by the animal's body.

2. Write another opinion from the paragraph.

_____

_____

_____

To parents   Go to page 121 and do Activity 3 with your child.

Exercise 11

Read the paragraph. Then follow the instructions.

Early Train Rides

The first railroad cars were scary. In the 1830s
passengers rode in cars that looked like
stagecoaches. Often showers of sparks
from the engine blew back
on them. That is so unsafe!
The crew on these early
trains didn't even ride
inside a car. If it rained or
snowed, they just got wet.
I would not have worked
on one of these trains.

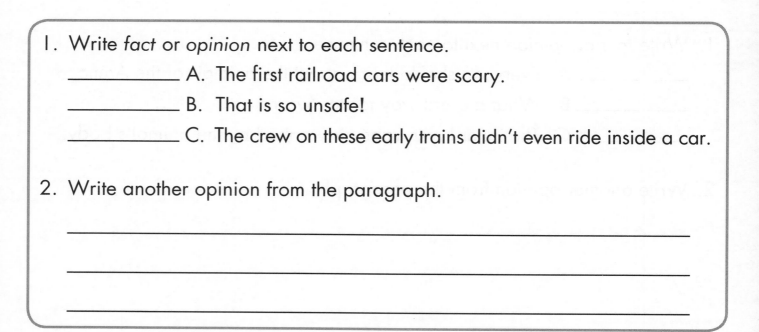

1. Write *fact* or *opinion* next to each sentence.

_____ A. The first railroad cars were scary.

_____ B. That is so unsafe!

_____ C. The crew on these early trains didn't even ride inside a car.

2. Write another opinion from the paragraph.

_____

_____

_____

To parents Go to page 121 and do Activity 3 with your child.

© 2013 Scholastic Education International (S) Pte Ltd ISBN 978-981-07-3287-5

Exercise 12

Read the paragraph. Then follow the instructions.

A Bird Story

Sometimes birds do unusual things. A bird in Pennsylvania spent hours looking in the mirror on the side of a car. Maybe it wasn't a very smart bird. The bird left scratches and dirt on the car. So the owner put a bag over the mirror when the car was parked. That was a clever way to solve the problem.

1. Write *fact* or *opinion* next to each sentence.

   _____ A. A bird in Pennsylvania spent hours looking in the mirror on the side of a car.

   _____ B. The bird left scratches and dirt on the car.

   _____ C. That was a clever way to solve the problem.

2. Write another fact from the paragraph.

   _____

   _____

   _____

To parents Go to page 121 and do Activity 3 with your child.

Exercise 13

Read the paragraph. Then follow the instructions.

Gray Whales

Gray whales spend their winters in warm waters off Mexico. I think that's very smart of them. The females have their young and nurse them during this time. By late spring the whales begin swimming north. They travel about 5,000 miles to the waters of the Arctic. These are their feeding grounds. They eat tiny creatures that look like shrimp. Gray whales are really amazing.

1. Write *fact* or *opinion* next to each sentence.

   _____ A. I think that's very smart of them.

   _____ B. The females have their young and nurse them during this time.

   _____ C. They travel about 5,000 miles to the waters of the Arctic.

2. Write another opinion from the paragraph.

   _____

   _____

   _____

To parents Go to page 121 and do Activity 3 with your child.

© 2013 Scholastic Education International (S) Pte Ltd ISBN 978-981-07-3287-5

Exercise 14

Read the paragraph. Then follow the instructions.

In the Shell

When a chick is in its shell, it needs air to breathe. The air seeps through tiny holes in the shell. Then the air passes through a thin skin inside the shell. Blood vessels carry the air to the chick. At one end of the shell is an air bubble. When the chick is ready to hatch, it pops this bubble. Then it practises using its lungs to breathe. Chicks look funny when they hatch.

1. Write *fact* or *opinion* next to each sentence.

    _____ A. The air seeps through tiny holes in the shell.

    _____ B. Blood vessels carry the air to the chick.

    _____ C. Chicks look funny when they hatch.

2. Write another fact from the paragraph.

    _____

    _____

    _____

To parents   Go to page 121 and do Activity 3 with your child.

© 2013 Scholastic Education International (S) Pte Ltd ISBN 978-981-07-3287-5

Exercise 15

Read the paragraph. Then follow the instructions.

Different Customs

People in other lands have some strange
customs. I would like to live in South Korea.
It's good manners to slurp soup there. I think
slurping soup shows that you like it. My mother
says it is impolite. In South Korea it is also good
manners to burp. I love the idea. A good slurp and
a good burp are fine with me.

1. Write *fact* or *opinion* next to each sentence.

    _____ A. I would like to live in South Korea.

    _____ B. It's good manners to slurp soup there.

    _____ C. I think slurping soup shows that you like it.

2. Write another opinion from the paragraph.

    _____

    _____

    _____

To parents   Go to page 121 and do Activity 3 with your child.

Exercise 16

Read the paragraph. Then follow the instructions.

Cloth for Clothes

People wear clothes made of cotton, wool, silk, and many other materials. Silk is the best. Now a scientist has invented cloth with tiny wires in it. This cloth can pick up signals from the wearer's body. I think this is very exciting. For example, the cloth can tell what a person's temperature is. If the wearer is sick, the cloth can send a signal to a computer to call for help.

1. Write *fact* or *opinion* next to each sentence.
   _____ A. Silk is the best.
   _____ B. Now a scientist has invented cloth with tiny wires in it.
   _____ C. This cloth can pick up signals from the wearer's body.

2. Write another opinion from the paragraph.

   _____

   _____

   _____

To parents   Go to page 121 and do Activity 3 with your child.

Exercise 17

Read the paragraph. Then follow the instructions.

Measure by Measure

People and horses are measured for height in different ways. People are measured from head to toe. But horses move their heads up and down a lot. It is hard to get a fixed measurement, so horses are measured from their feet to their withers. The withers are on a horse's back above the shoulders. You should remember this to tell your friends.

1. Write *fact* or *opinion* next to each sentence.

   _____ A. People are measured from head to toe.

   _____ B. But horses move their heads up and down a lot.

   _____ C. You should remember this to tell your friends.

2. Write another fact from the paragraph.

   _____

   _____

   _____

To parents Go to page 121 and do Activity 3 with your child.

Exercise 18

Read the paragraph. Then follow the instructions.

Behind Bars

Oriental pied hornbills are protective and
caring parents. During the breeding season,
the female hornbill nests in a tree hole. She
seals the entrance to the hole with a mixture
of saliva, stool, clay and rotten wood. The
male will pass food to her through a slit. This
keeps the babies safe from enemies. As the
babies grow, the babies reseal the entrance
themselves when mother hornbill flies off to get
them more food. What a great family!

1. Write *fact* or *opinion* next to each sentence.

   _____ A. Female hornbills seal the entrance to the tree hole.

   _____ B. Male hornbills pass food to the female through a slit.

   _____ C. Oriental pied hornbills are caring and protective parents.

2. Write another opinion from the paragraph.

   _____

   _____

   _____

© 2013 Scholastic Education International (S) Pte Ltd   ISBN 978-981-07-3287-5

Exercise 19

Read the paragraph. Then follow the instructions.

Yummy Bread

Bread forms an important part of our diet. Many people are familiar with sandwiches, pizzas, croissants, rolls and burgers. Eating bread is good for us. Bread gives us energy and helps us grow. It also contains minerals which are good for our teeth and blood. Bread is made mainly from flour, water and yeast. Bread makers are becoming more common and affordable so more people bake their own bread. Raisins, dried fruits, chocolates and even candies may be added to bread. Bread can be rather fanciful these days.

1. Write *fact* or *opinion* next to each sentence.

    _____ A. Bread can be rather fanciful these days.

    _____ B. Bread is made mainly from flour, water and yeast.

    _____ C. Bread gives us energy and helps us grow.

2. Write another opinion from the paragraph.

    _____

    _____

    _____

To parents Go to page 121 and do Activity 3 with your child.

Exercise 20

Read the paragraph. Then follow the instructions.

Rainbows

A rainbow is a beautiful natural phenomenon. It appears in the sky when the sun shines after a rain. Although sunlight looks white, it actually consists of many colors. When it shines on raindrops, the raindrops cause the light to split up into different colors. Some people do not include indigo as a separate color, therefore they say a rainbow only has six colors. I think a rainbow has seven colors – red, orange, yellow, green, indigo, blue and violet.

1. Write *fact* or *opinion* next to each sentence.

   _____ A. A rainbow may appear in the sky after a rain.

   _____ B. A rainbow is a beautiful natural phenomenon.

   _____ C. Raindrops cause the light to split up into different colors.

2. Write another opinion from the paragraph.

   _____

   _____

   _____

To parents Go to page 121 and do Activity 3 with your child.

Exercise 21

Read the paragraph. Then follow the instructions.

Dogs Make Good Pets

I think dogs make good pets. Dogs are fantastic and loyal
companions. When their masters are feeling down, they will
lie faithfully at their feet, offering a listening ear. Dogs are
also great protectors. They are protective of their masters.
They will be in the attackers' face if someone or an animal
threatens to attack their masters.
People sometimes keep dogs to
guard their houses. Dogs are easy to
care for. A daily pat on the head, a
bath and a walk can win the loyalty
of an animal who thinks the world
of you.

1. Write *fact* or *opinion* next to each sentence.

    _____ A. I think dogs make good pets.

    _____ B. Dogs are fantastic and loyal companions.

    _____ C. Dogs are easy to care for.

2. Write another fact from the paragraph.

    _____

    _____

    _____

To parents   Go to page 121 and do Activity 3 with your child.

© 2013 Scholastic Education International (S) Pte Ltd ISBN 978-981-07-3287-5

Exercise 22

Read the paragraph. Then follow the instructions.

Roll All the Way

Early man relied on his own strength to carry objects. Over the years, people tamed animals such as oxen, donkeys and horses to help them. However, there was still a limit to the amount of goods an animal could carry. That prompted the idea of sledges that could be pulled by animals. In places where sledges were not suitable, such

as on rough ground, men attached sections of logs to heavy objects and rolled them to various places. The wheel was thus born. What a terrific invention!

1. Write *fact* or *opinion* next to each sentence.

_____ A. Early man relied on his own strength to carry objects.

_____ B. The wheel was a terrific invention.

_____ C. An animal could not carry too many heavy things on its back.

2. Write another fact from the paragraph.

_____

_____

_____

To parents   Go to page 121 and do Activity 3 with your child.

Exercise 23

Read the paragraph. Then follow the instructions.

Do you have a Pouch too?

Most marsupials live in the Americas or Australasia. They include kangaroos, ningauis, opossums and koalas. They live in many different environments such as forests, plains and deserts. The young of marsupials spend most of their time in their mothers' pouches. This is because the newborn of a marsupial is normally born immature and has to be nourished by its mother's milk. The pouch of a female marsupial protects its baby. What a comfort! I wish I could stay in Mummy's pouch for a long, long time too.

1. Write *fact* or *opinion* next to each sentence.

   _____ A. The newborn of a marsupial is normally born immature.

   _____ B. Marsupials include kangaroos, ningauis, opossums and koalas.

   _____ C. I wish I could stay in Mummy's pouch for a long, long time too.

2. Write another opinion from the paragraph.

   _____

   _____

   _____

To parents   Go to page 121 and do Activity 3 with your child.

Exercise 24

Read the paragraph. Then follow the instructions.

Mid-Autumn Festival

Mid-Autumn Festival is a Chinese festival. Eating mooncakes is one of the popular celebrations of the day. Mooncakes are traditional Chinese pastries made of wheat flour and sweet stuffing. I love eating mooncakes. Mooncakes symbolize family reunion, and are traditionally cut into pieces that equal the number of family members. During the 14th century, mooncakes acted like our modern e-mails. Rebels hid important notes in mooncakes to spread the message of the revolution wide and far. That was a smart way to communicate.

1. Write *fact* or *opinion* next to each sentence.

   _____ A. Mooncakes symbolize family reunion.

   _____ B. I love eating mooncakes.

   _____ C. Rebels hid important notes in mooncakes to spread the message of the revolution wide and far.

2. Write another opinion from the paragraph.

   _____

   _____

   _____

To parents Go to page 121 and do Activity 3 with your child.

Exercise 25

Read the paragraph. Then follow the instructions.

Animal Homes

Animals live in many different types of homes. Wild animals build their own homes but farm animals live in special homes constructed by farmers. Rabbits build tunnels called warrens. These tunnels lead to an underground nest. A rabbit's home is like a maze. This helps the rabbit escape in times of danger. Rabbits must be clever to devise such an intricate home security system.

1. Write *fact* or *opinion* next to each sentence.

   _____ A. Rabbits must be clever to devise such an intricate home security system.

   _____ B. Rabbits build underground tunnels called warrens.

   _____ C. Farm animals live in special homes constructed by farmers.

2. Write another opinion from the paragraph.

   _____

   _____

   _____

To parents Go to page 121 and do Activity 3 with your child.

© 2013 Scholastic Education International (S) Pte Ltd ISBN 978-981-07-3287-5

Exercise 26

Read the paragraph. Then follow the instructions.

Football

Football is one of the most popular sports in Europe and America. It is more than just a game of chasing a ball across the field. Becoming a football star is a dream of many youngsters. Many talented players earn a huge amount of money playing football professionally. These men do not have any other job except to play football for a team or a club. This must be a fun way to work!

1. Write *fact* or *opinion* next to each sentence.

   _____ A. Football is one of the most popular sports in Europe and America.

   _____ B. Many talented players earn a huge amount of money playing football professionally.

   _____ C. This must be a fun way to work!

2. Write another fact from the paragraph.

   _____

   _____

   _____

To parents   Go to page 121 and do Activity 3 with your child.

Exercise 27

Read the paragraph. Then follow the instructions.

Polar Bears

Polar bears belong to the bear family. They are the most amazing of all bears. They live in places like Alaska, Canada and other countries in the polar region. Polar bears are carnivorous. They eat seals, which they catch through holes in ice. The polar bear's coat is long and white. There are two layers to it. The outer coat helps the bear shakes off water and snow. The fur underneath keeps it warm. What a practical way to stay warm in the cold region!

1. Write *fact* or *opinion* next to each sentence.

   _____ A. Polar bears are carnivorous.

   _____ B. The polar bears coat is long and white.

   _____ C. What a practical way to stay warm in the cold region!

2. Write another opinion from the paragraph.

   _____

   _____

   _____

To parents Go to page 121 and do Activity 3 with your child.

Exercise 28

Read the paragraph. Then follow the instructions.

Excuse Me, I am Taken!

Many places have their own unique ways to reserve seats. Singapore has its own creative way too. During lunch hour, packets of tissues on chairs are a common sight in food centers. Before heading off to the different stalls to purchase their lunch, people often leave packets of tissues on chairs. This is to tell others that the seats have been taken. This is an unspoken social rule respected by those who work in the area. In my opinion, this is a practical way to reserve seats.

1. Write *fact* or *opinion* next to each sentence.

   _____ A. Singapore has its own creative way too.

   _____ B. During lunch hour, packets of tissues on chairs are a common sight in food centers.

   _____ C. This is an unspoken social rule respected by those who work in the area.

2. Write another opinion from the paragraph.

   _____

   _____

   _____

To parents   Go to page 121 and do Activity 3 with your child.

© 2013 Scholastic Education International (S) Pte Ltd   ISBN 978-981-07-3287-5

Exercise 29

Read the paragraph. Then follow the instructions.

Saturn

Scientists have been fascinated by the planets in our solar system for many years. Saturn is a gas planet and the second largest. It is by far the most beautiful planet because it is surrounded by a spectacular ring system that stretches out into space. The rings are made up of millions of ice crystals as huge as houses or as small as specks of dust. I wish human beings could travel to Saturn one day.

1. Write *fact* or *opinion* next to each sentence.

   _____ A. Saturn is a gas planet and the second largest.

   _____ B. Saturn is the most beautiful planet.

   _____ C. I wish human beings could travel to Saturn one day.

2. Write another opinion from the paragraph.

   _____

   _____

   _____

To parents Go to page 121 and do Activity 3 with your child.

Comparing and Contrasting

Making comparisons is an essential reading comprehension skill that enriches a reader's understanding of the text. A reader who can compare and contrast events, characters, places, and facts is able to identify similarities and differences, and to categorize or group information. The passages and questions in this section will help your child learn to compare and contrast.

This section will provide opportunities for your child to understand that comparing and contrasting helps him to organize and comprehend information in the text. This is essential especially as your child encounters more non-fiction texts.

The extension activities provide additional challenges to your child to encourage and develop his understanding of the particular comprehension skill.

© 2013 Scholastic Education International (S) Pte Ltd ISBN 978-981-07-3287-5

Exercise 1

Read the paragraph. Then answer the questions.

Polly and I

My twin sister, Polly, and I are alike in many ways. We both have long, straight hair, dimples and love to smile. Mummy says our limbs are so long that we look like two adorable monkeys. Polly and I have our differences too. Polly likes to wear T-shirts and pants. I like to wear dresses. Polly enjoys all kinds of sports but I like to draw. When Polly grows up, she wants to be an astronaut. When I grow up, I want to be an artist.

1. How are the twins alike?

    ○ A. They love to smile.

    ○ B. They want to be teachers when they grow up.

    ○ C. They love to eat spaghetti.

2. How are the twins different?

    ○ A. Polly likes to read.

    ○ B. Polly enjoys all kind of sports.

    ○ C. Polly has long limbs.

3. Write another way that the twins are different.

    _____

    _____

    _____

    _____

    _____

    _____

To parents   Go to page 122 and do Activity 4 with your child.

Exercise 2

Read the paragraph. Then answer the questions.

Am I an Insect?

Is a spider an insect? Spiders belong to the arachnid family. They are predators. They spin webs and capture their prey. A spider has two body parts and eight legs. An insect, on the other hand, has three body parts and six legs. Most insects have wings and feelers, but spiders do not. Both insects and spiders, however, have a hard covering, called an exoskeleton, on the outside to protect and support their bodies. Both insects and spiders hatch from eggs.

1. How are spiders and insects alike?
   ○ A. They have exoskeletons.
   ○ B. They have wings.
   ○ C. They spin webs.

2. How are spiders and insects different?
   ○ A. Spiders are bigger than insects.
   ○ B. Spiders and insects are anthropods.
   ○ C. A spider has two body parts and eight legs.

3. Write another way that spiders and insects are alike.

   _____

   _____

   _____

   _____

   _____

To parents   Go to page 122 and do Activity 4 with your child.

Exercise 3

Read the paragraph. Then answer the questions.

Meet Two Dogs

Meet Aibo and Fido. Aibo is a dog. But he is also a robot. Aibo is expensive — he costs $2,500. Many people like this metal pet. He comes when he's called, and he doesn't need to be walked. Fido is a mutt, but he's a real dog. His furry coat sometimes sheds. His owner must take him out twice a day. Fido's owner got him for free from an animal shelter. Both Aibo and Fido have learned to do tricks.

1. How are the dogs alike?
   - ○ A. They cost a lot of money.
   - ○ B. They are someone's pets.
   - ○ C. They are both mutts.

2. How are the dogs different?
   - ○ A. Fido can do tricks.
   - ○ B. Aibo is made of metal.
   - ○ C. Aibo needs to be walked.

3. Write another way that the dogs are alike.

   _____

   _____

   _____

   _____

   _____

To parents Go to page 122 and do Activity 4 with your child.

© 2013 Scholastic Education International (S) Pte Ltd ISBN 978-981-07-3287-5

Exercise 4

Read the paragraph. Then answer the questions.

Birds and Turtles

Mother birds lay eggs in nests where they are safe. Little birds hatch from the eggs. They cheep and cheep until their parents bring them food. Turtles lay eggs, too. Mother turtles lay their eggs in the sand where the eggs will be safe. But mother turtles cover the eggs and leave. When it is time, small turtles hatch from the eggs. They dig their way up and learn to find food on their own.

1. How are birds and turtles alike?
   - ○ A. They have hard shells.
   - ○ B. The young hatch from eggs.
   - ○ C. The mothers leave the eggs.

2. How are birds and turtles different?
   - ○ A. Bird parents feed their young.
   - ○ B. They lay eggs in safe places.
   - ○ C. The young need food to eat.

3. Write another way that bird eggs and turtle eggs are different.

   _____

   _____

   _____

   _____

   _____

To parents   Go to page 122 and do Activity 4 with your child.

Exercise 5

Read the paragraph. Then answer the questions.

Two Kinds of Cats

Leopards and lions are two kinds of wild cats. Both are big meat eaters that hunt other animals for food. Leopards have thick golden-yellow fur coats covered with dark spots. They are very good climbers. They often take their food up into trees for dinner. Leopards like to be alone. Lions are more than twice the size of leopards. These tan cats live together in groups called prides.

1. How are leopards and lions alike?
   - ○ A. They eat meat.
   - ○ B. They have spots.
   - ○ C. They live in prides.

2. How are leopards and lions different?
   - ○ A. They are hunters.
   - ○ B. Lions are bigger.
   - ○ C. Leopards are cats.

3. Write another way that leopards and lions are alike.

   _____
   _____
   _____
   _____
   _____

To parents Go to page 122 and do Activity 4 with your child.

© 2013 Scholastic Education International (S) Pte Ltd ISBN 978-981-07-3287-5

Exercise 6

Read the paragraph. Then answer the questions.

Which Is It?

Is it a butterfly or a moth? Both belong to the same group of insects. Both have wings and feelers called antennae. But most butterflies hold their wings up when they land. Most moths keep their wings flat. Butterflies are usually active during the day. Moths are usually busy at night. The antennae on a butterfly have knobs on the end. Moths do not have these.

1. How are butterflies and moths alike?
   - ○ A. They have antennae.
   - ○ B. They hold their wings up.
   - ○ C. They are active at night.

2. How are butterflies and moths different?
   - ○ A. Moths do not have knobs on their antennae.
   - ○ B. Butterflies belong to a different insect group.
   - ○ C. Butterflies have bigger wings than moths.

3. Write another way that moths and butterflies are alike.

   _____

   _____

   _____

   _____

   _____

   _____

To parents   Go to page 122 and do Activity 4 with your child.

Exercise 7

Read the paragraph. Then answer the questions.

Surfing

Surfing is a popular sport in oceans and the Great Lakes. It takes a stormy day for good waves to build on the lakes. Usually lake surfers go out in the winter. They wear long wetsuits to keep warm in the cold waters. Ocean surfers can count on good waves much more often. They can usually wear just bathing suits and surf in sunny weather. Surfers use a board for both lake and ocean surfing.

1. How are lake and ocean surfing alike?

   ○ A. They wear wetsuits.

   ○ B. They use a board on the waves.

   ○ C. They can count on good waves.

2. How are lake and ocean surfing different?

   ○ A. Lake surfers usually wear bathing suits.

   ○ B. The sport is popular in both kinds of water.

   ○ C. Lake waves build only in stormy weather.

3. Write another way that lake and ocean surfing are different.

   _____

   _____

   _____

   _____

   _____

   _____

To parents   Go to page 122 and do Activity 4 with your child.

© 2013 Scholastic Education International (S) Pte Ltd ISBN 978-981-07-3287-5

Exercise 8

Read the paragraph. Then answer the questions.

Racing Cars

Have you ever seen a racing car? Formula One cars race on tracks. These are high-powered cars that go very fast. They have specially made bodies and engines. Stock cars are regular cars that have been changed for racing. These cars go fast but not as fast as Formula One racers. Stock cars usually race on tracks too.

1. How are Formula One cars and stock cars alike?

   ○ A. They have specially made engines.

   ○ B. They are made from regular cars.

   ○ C. They are used for races on tracks.

2. How are Formula One cars and stock cars different?

   ○ A. They use a parachute to stop them.

   ○ B. Formula One cars go faster.

   ○ C. Stock cars have specially made bodies.

3. Write another way that Formula One cars and stock cars are different.

   _____

   _____

   _____

   _____

   _____

   _____

To parents   Go to page 122 and do Activity 4 with your child.

Exercice 9

Read the paragraph. Then answer the questions.

Babirusa and Warthog

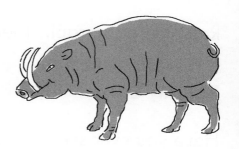

Warthogs and babirusas are two kinds of bizarre looking wild pigs. Both live in family groups of a female and her young and have unusual tusks. However, all the tusks of a warthog grow from the side of its mouth. The upper tusks of a babirusa, in contrast, grow through the top of its snout. Babirusas are found in the rainforests of West Sulawesi, Indonesia. Warthogs are found in the grasslands and woodlands of Africa.

1. How are warthogs and babirusas alike?

   ○ A. They are found in the same country.

   ○ B. They are both wild pigs.

   ○ C. They are kept for meat.

2. How are warthogs and babirusas different?

   ○ A. Warthogs live in family groups of a female and her young.

   ○ B. The upper tusks of a babirusa grow through the top of its snout.

   ○ C. Babirusas look weird.

3. Write another way that warthogs and babirusas are different.

   _____

   _____

   _____

   _____

   _____

   _____

To parents Go to page 122 and do Activity 4 with your child.

Exercise 10

Read the paragraph. Then answer the questions.

Jasmine's and Crystal's Goldfish

Both Jasmine and Crystal have goldfish. They put their goldfish in a fish tank. Jasmine put seaweed, colorful pebbles and a water pump in her tank. Jasmine changes the water in her fish tank weekly and feeds her fish once a day. Occasionally, she gives her fish a special treat — worms. Crystal was very excited to have goldfish too. However, she always forgets to feed her fish. Her fish tank smells because she finds changing the water in her fish bowl a chore.

1. How are Jasmine's and Crystal's goldfish alike?

   ○ A. They love to eat worms.

   ○ B. They have fresh water every week.

   ○ C. They live in fish tanks.

2. How are Jasmine's and Crystal's fish tanks different?

   ○ A. Crystal's has water.

   ○ B. Jasmine's has colorful pebbles, seaweed and a water pump.

   ○ C. Jasmine's fish tank is made of plastic.

3. Write another way in which the girls treat the goldfish differently.

   _____

   _____

   _____

   _____

   _____

   _____

To parents Go to page 122 and do Activity 4 with your child.

Exercise 11

Read the paragraph. Then answer the questions.

All About Bears

Bears have poor eyesight. They have poor hearing too. Instead, they use their sense of smell to find food. Brown bears are called grizzly bears because of white hairs in their fur. Brown bears eat plants. Sometimes they eat fish or other animals. Polar bears eat only meat. They have white fur and live in the Arctic. Polar bears have special cups on the soles of their feet to keep them from sliding on ice. These bears are bigger than brown bears.

1. How are brown bears and polar bears alike?

   ○ A. They eat only plants.

   ○ B. They have white fur.

   ○ C. They have poor hearing.

2. How are brown bears and polar bears different?

   ○ A. Polar bears have a good sense of smell.

   ○ B. Polar bears eat other animals for food.

   ○ C. Brown bears are called grizzlies.

3. Write another way that brown bears and polar bears are alike.

   _____

   _____

   _____

   _____

   _____

   _____

To parents   Go to page 122 and do Activity 4 with your child.

© 2013 Scholastic Education International (S) Pte Ltd ISBN 978-981-07-3287-5

Exercise 12

Read the paragraph. Then answer the questions.

Looking at Leaves

The leaves on trees are not all alike. Some leaves have jagged edges called teeth. Toothed leaves can be oval, skinny, or shaped like a heart. Beech and elm trees have such leaves. Other trees have leaves shaped like a hand with the fingers spread out. These leaves have three to seven fingers or lobes. Many maple trees have such leaves. Both types of leaves drop off trees in the fall.

1. How are toothed leaves and hand-shaped leaves alike?

   ○ A. They grow on trees.

   ○ B. They have lobes.

   ○ C. They have teeth.

2. How are toothed leaves and hand-shaped leaves different?

   ○ A. Maple leaves drop off in the fall.

   ○ B. Elm leaves are shaped like hands.

   ○ C. Toothed leaves have jagged edges.

3. Write another way that toothed leaves and hand-shaped leaves are alike.

   _____

   _____

   _____

   _____

   _____

   _____

To parents   Go to page 122 and do Activity 4 with your child.

Date: _____

Exercise 13

Read the paragraph. Then answer the questions.

Play Ball

Baseball and basketball are both played with balls. In baseball the players hit the ball with a bat. In basketball the players toss the ball through a hoop. Both sports are played with teams. A basketball team has five players, while a baseball team has nine. In baseball the way to score is to get runs. Basketball players try to get goals. In both sports the team with the higher score wins.

1. How are baseball and basketball alike?
   - ○ A. They have five players.
   - ○ B. They are team sports.
   - ○ C. The ball goes through a hoop.

2. How are baseball and basketball different?
   - ○ A. The highest scoring team wins.
   - ○ B. Baseball players hit the ball with a bat.
   - ○ C. Basketball is played with a ball.

3. Write another way that baseball and basketball are different.

   _____

   _____

   _____

   _____

   _____

   _____

To parents Go to page 122 and do Activity 4 with your child.

Exercise 14

Read the paragraph. Then answer the questions.

Frogs and Toads

People often confuse frogs and toads. Both are amphibians. This means they are cold-blooded; their temperature stays the same as their surroundings. Frogs and toads have four legs and no tails. They use their back legs for jumping. The legs on frogs are longer. Toads have drier, lumpier skin. Most adult frogs live in or near water. Most adult toads live on land.

1. How are frogs and toads alike?

   ○ A. They live mostly on land.

   ○ B. They are cold-blooded.

   ○ C. They have long tails.

2. How are frogs and toads different?

   ○ A. Toads jump with their back legs.

   ○ B. Toads live mostly on land.

   ○ C. Frogs have lumpier skin.

3. Write another way that frogs and toads are alike.

   _____

   _____

   _____

   _____

   _____

To parents   Go to page 122 and do Activity 4 with your child.

© 2013 Scholastic Education International (S) Pte Ltd   ISBN 978-981-07-3287-5

Exercise 15

Read the paragraph. Then answer the questions.

All about Emergency Vehicles

Fire engines and ambulances help to rescue people. They bring firefighters and paramedics to places quickly. They usually have loud sirens and flashing lights to alert road users. A fire engine can carry many firefighters. It has a tool box and a water tanker. An ambulance carries a variety of medical supplies and equipment. The ambulance usually has room for one or more patients and several paramedics.

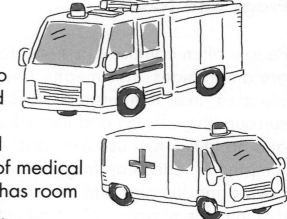

1. How are fire engines and ambulances alike?
   - ○ A. They bring firefighters and paramedics to places quickly.
   - ○ B. They carry water tanker.
   - ○ C. They are usually red.

2. How are fire engines and ambulances different?
   - ○ A. Ambulances help to rescue people.
   - ○ B. Fire engines have loud sirens and flashing lights.
   - ○ C. An ambulance has room for patients and paramedics.

3. Write another way that fire engines and ambulances are alike.

   _____

   _____

   _____

   _____

   _____

To parents   Go to page 122 and do Activity 4 with your child.

106   © 2013 Scholastic Education International (S) Pte Ltd ISBN 978-981-07-3287-5

Exercise 16

Read the paragraph. Then answer the questions.

Click Click

My big brother has a digital camera and a computer. He takes photographs with his digital camera and sends e-mails with his computer. He uses both his digital camera and his computer for his school projects. He takes photographs on his camera and downloads them into his computer. He types his reports on his computer. Both the digital camera and computer have a monitor to show the user what he is doing. They may also have a microphone and speakers.

1. How are computers and digital cameras alike?
   - ○ A. They are used to take photographs.
   - ○ B. They have a monitor to show the user what he is doing.
   - ○ C. They are used for typing.

2. How are computers and digital cameras different?
   - ○ A. My brother uses his computer to type his school projects.
   - ○ B. The digital camera has a monitor.
   - ○ C. A computer has a microphone and speakers.

3. Write another way that computers and digital cameras are different.

   _____

   _____

   _____

   _____

   _____

   _____

To parents Go to page 122 and do Activity 4 with your child.

Exercise 17

Read the paragraph. Then answer the questions.

Life in Space

Astronauts work, travel and live in a spaceship while they are in space. Unlike on Earth, astronauts float around in space due to the lack of gravity. They even sleep with seat belts on to avoid knocking into objects. Astronauts eat foods similar to what we eat on Earth. However, their foods must be freeze-dried, pre-cooked or dehydrated. If food is dehydrated, it cannot be eaten until the astronauts add hot water to it. Astronauts use a toothbrush to brush their teeth, just like they would on land.

1. How is living on earth and in space alike?

   ○ A. Astronauts use a toothbrush to brush their teeth.

   ○ B. Food must be freeze-dried, pre-cooked or dehydrated.

   ○ C. Astronauts walk on Earth.

2. How is living on earth and in space different?

   ○ A. Astronauts eat similar foods.

   ○ B. Astronauts travel in aeroplanes.

   ○ C. Astronauts float around in space.

3. Write another way that living on earth and living in space are alike.

   _____

   _____

   _____

   _____

   _____

   _____

To parents Go to page 122 and do Activity 4 with your child.

108

Exercise 18

Read the paragraph. Then answer the questions.

Whale Tales

Whales live all their lives in water. These large mammals are very smart. The blue whale is the biggest mammal of all. Both the blue whale and the humpback whale are baleen whales. They have no teeth. Instead they have baleen, or thin plates, in their mouth to strain out food. The humpback whale is black with white on it. This whale has long flippers. The blue whale is a blue-gray color.

1. How are blue whales and humpback whales alike?

   ○ A. They are black and white.

   ○ B. They have long flippers.

   ○ C. They are both mammals.

2. How are blue whales and humpback whales different?

   ○ A. The humpback is a baleen whale.

   ○ B. The blue whale is very smart.

   ○ C. The blue whale is larger.

3. Write another way that the blue whale and the humpback whale are alike.

   _____

   _____

   _____

   _____

   _____

   _____

To parents   Go to page 122 and do Activity 4 with your child.

Exercise 19

Read the paragraph. Then answer the questions.

Strike Up the Band

When a band plays, you hear brass instruments. The players make different sounds by blowing into a mouthpiece. A trumpet player presses valves to change the sound. A trombone player pulls a slide back and forth. The trumpet has a higher sound than the trombone. The trombone is a larger instrument.

1. How are the trumpet and the trombone alike?

   ○ A. The players pull a slide back and forth.

   ○ B. The players blow into a mouthpiece.

   ○ C. They are of the same size.

2. How are the trumpet and the trombone different?

   ○ A. The trombone has a lower sound.

   ○ B. The trumpet is played in bands.

   ○ C. The trombone is a brass instrument.

3. Write another way that the trumpet and trombone are different.

   _____

   _____

   _____

   _____

   _____

To parents   Go to page 122 and do Activity 4 with your child.

Exercise 20

Read the paragraph. Then answer the questions.

The Big Bad Wolf

Two popular tales for children are *Little Red Riding Hood* and *The Boy Who Cried Wolf.* Both tales have a big bad wolf. The wolf is a scary character that eats humans or sheep. In *The Boy Who Cried Wolf,* the boy lies to his neighbors so many times that no one believes him when the wolf really comes. In *Little Red Riding Hood* however, her cries for help are heard and a woodcutter comes to her rescue.

1. How are the stories alike?
   - ○ A. They are about sheep.
   - ○ B. They are about lying to others.
   - ○ C. They involve a wolf.

2. How are the stories different?
   - ○ A. *Little Red Riding Hood* is popular.
   - ○ B. The wolf is a scary character.
   - ○ C. The boy does not get the help he needs.

3. Write another way that the stories are alike.

   _____

   _____

   _____

   _____

   _____

   _____

To parents Go to page 122 and do Activity 4 with your child.

Exercise 21

Read the paragraph. Then answer the questions.

Olympics Now and Then

The Olympics is considered the most important sports competition. The essence of the Games is not to win but to take part. The Games began over 2,700 years ago. In the past, only men were allowed to participate and the Olympics were held only in Greece. Now, both men and women can compete and the Olympics are held in various cities in the world. Winners received a crown of olive leaves back then, but winners receive a gold, silver or bronze medal now.

1. How are the Olympics in the past and present alike?
   - ○ A. Women can compete in the games.
   - ○ B. It is considered the most important sports competition.
   - ○ C. They are held in Greece.

2. How are the Olympics in the past and present different?
   - ○ A. Winners received a crown of olive leaves back then.
   - ○ B. The essence of the Games is not to win but to take part.
   - ○ C. Only women could compete in the past.

3. Write another way that the Olympics in the past and present are different.

   _____
   _____
   _____
   _____
   _____
   _____

To parents   Go to page 122 and do Activity 4 with your child.

Exercise 22

Read the paragraph. Then answer the questions.

What Am I?

Alligators and crocodiles are reptiles.
They have scaly skins and lay eggs. They
have long tails, short legs and sharp teeth.
Although alligators and crocodiles may
look alike, we can tell their difference by
looking at their snouts. Most alligators have round snouts while most crocodiles
have pointed snouts. Unlike a crocodile, the teeth of an alligator do not stick out
when its jaws are closed. Alligators live only in the United States and China, but
crocodiles can be found in different parts of the world.

1. How are alligators and crocodiles alike?

   ○ A. They live in Australia.

   ○ B. They are reptiles.

   ○ C. Their teeth stick out when their jaws are closed.

2. How are alligators and crocodiles different?

   ○ A. They are animals.

   ○ B. Most crocodiles have pointed snouts.

   ○ C. Alligators can be found in many countries.

3. Write another way that alligators and crocodiles are alike.

   _____

   _____

   _____

   _____

   _____

   _____

To parents   Go to page 122 and do Activity 4 with your child.

© 2013 Scholastic Education International (S) Pte Ltd ISBN 978-981-07-3287-5

Exercise 23

Read the paragraph. Then answer the questions.

Public and Private Transportation

Public and private vehicles help bring us to our destinations. Public transport includes taxis, buses, aeroplanes, trains and ferries. Private transport refers to cars, motorcycles and bicycles. We have to pay a fare to travel on it. In contrast, we do not have to pay a fare or share with strangers when taking private transport. Public transport does not require the users to clean or maintain the vehicle.

1. How are public transport and private transport alike?

   ○ A. They help bring us to our destinations.

   ○ B. We have to pay a fare.

   ○ C. Buses, taxis and trains are public transport.

2. How are public transport and private transport different?

   ○ A. Buses, taxis and trains are private transport.

   ○ B. We have to pay a fare to travel on public transport.

   ○ C. They help bring us to our destinations.

3. Write another way that public transport and private transport are different.

   _____

   _____

   _____

   _____

   _____

   _____

To parents Go to page 122 and do Activity 4 with your child.

© 2013 Scholastic Education International (S) Pte Ltd ISBN 978-981-07-3287-5

Exercise 24

Read the paragraph. Then answer the questions.

Pygmy Hippos and Common Hippos

The word hippopotamus comes from two Greek words
for "river horse." Both pygmy hippos and common
hippos are mammals. They have smooth skin, with
almost no hair and are herbivores. Pygmy hippos are
much smaller than common hippos. Pygmy hippos live in
swamps while common hippos live in rivers and lakes.
The pygmy hippo is called the underwater ballerina. It
tiptoes along the riverbeds as it cannot swim and it is too dense to float.

1. How are pygmy hippos and
   common hippos alike?
   - ○ A. They are the same size.
   - ○ B. They live in zoos.
   - ○ C. They are mammals.

2. How are pygmy hippos and
   common hippos different?
   - ○ A. Pygmy hippos are
     meat-eaters.
   - ○ B. Pygmy hippos live
     in swamps.
   - ○ C. Common hippos have
     smooth skin.

3. Write another way that pygmy
   hippos and common hippos
   are alike.

   _____

   _____

   _____

   _____

   _____

To parents Go to page 122 and do Activity 4 with your child.

Exercise 25

Read the paragraph. Then answer the questions.

Winters and Summers

Winters and summers are seasons of the year.
They affect how we lead our daily lives such as the
food we eat, the clothes we wear and the activities
we take part in. During the winter months, the days
are usually shorter and colder. In some countries,
it may even snow. During the summer months, the
days are usually longer and warmer. Although we
can spend more time outside on sunny days, we
should not stay out too long in the sun as the sun's rays can harm our bodies.

1. How are winters and summers alike?
   - ○ A. They are seasons of the year.
   - ○ B. Children play at the beach during summer.
   - ○ C. There may be snow.

2. How are winters and summers different?
   - ○ A. They affect the activities we take part in.
   - ○ B. My sister loves winter.
   - ○ C. Days are longer and warmer during summer.

3. Write another way that winters and summers are different.

   _____

   _____

   _____

   _____

   _____

   _____

To parents Go to page 122 and do Activity 4 with your child.

© 2013 Scholastic Education International (S) Pte Ltd ISBN 978-981-07-3287-5

Exercise 26

Read the paragraph. Then answer the questions.

David and Daphne's Ambitions

Both David and Daphne want to help people when they grow up. David wants to be a firefighter while Daphne wants to be a nurse. They have had their ambitions ever since they attended Career Day. David admires firefighters because they are brave, smart and help people in danger. Daphne admires nurses because they are brave, kind and take good care of the sick. Daphne is a member of the Red Cross Society while David is a member of the Civil Defence Club.

1. How are David and Daphne's ambitions alike?

   ○ A. They want to be nurses.

   ○ B. They are in the Red Cross Society.

   ○ C. They help people.

2. How are David and Daphne's ambitions different?

   ○ A. David has had that ambition ever since Career Day.

   ○ B. Nurses take care of the sick.

   ○ C. They are brave.

3. Write another way that David and Daphne's ambitions are alike.

   _____

   _____

   _____

   _____

   _____

   _____

To parents   Go to page 122 and do Activity 4 with your child.

Exercise 27

Read the paragraph. Then answer the questions.

Different Types of Homes

Igloos and huts are types of homes. Igloos provide cozy homes for the Inuit. They are built using ice. The inside of the igloo is lined with animal skins. The Inuit build a fire in the igloo to provide light and warmth. Huts provide temporary shelter for the nomads. They are built of readily available materials such as ice, stone, grass, branches and mud. Some huts can be moved easily and can withstand different weather conditions.

1. How are igloos and huts alike?

   ○ A. They can be moved easily.

   ○ B. They are types of homes.

   ○ C. They are cold on the outside.

2. How are igloos and huts different?

   ○ A. Igloos are built using ice and lined with animal skins.

   ○ B. They provide shelter for people.

   ○ C. Igloos can withstand most weather conditions.

3. Write another way that igloos and huts are different.

   _____

   _____

   _____

   _____

   _____

   _____

To parents Go to page 122 and do Activity 4 with your child.

© 2013 Scholastic Education International (S) Pte Ltd ISBN 978-981-07-3287-5

Exercise 28

Read the paragraph. Then answer the questions.

Meat-eating Plants

Pitcher Plants and Venus Flytraps are carnivorous plants. They live in wet places with poor soil conditions. They eat insects for nutrients. Pitcher Plants are shaped like tall glasses. Many insects are attracted to the sweet-smelling liquid in the pouch of the Pitcher Plant. The insects are dissolved by the liquid and absorbed by the plant. Venus Flytraps have big, sensitive leaves with spikes around their edges. When an insect lands on a leaf, it snaps shut, trapping the insect inside it.

1. How are Pitcher Plants and Venus Flytraps alike?

   ○ A. They live in places with poor soil nutrients.

   ○ B. They eat other plants.

   ○ C. They dissolve insects.

2. How are Pitcher Plants and Venus Flytraps different?

   ○ A. They eat insects.

   ○ B. Venus Flytraps have spikes on the edges of its leaves.

   ○ C. Venus Flytraps live in wet places.

3. Write another way that Pitcher Plants and Venus Flytraps are alike.

   _____

   _____

   _____

   _____

   _____

   _____

To parents   Go to page 122 and do Activity 4 with your child.

Exercise 29

Read the paragraph. Then answer the questions.

Animals in the Cold

Penguins and Arctic foxes live in extremely cold regions. Penguins live in the Antarctic (South Pole). They have short wings and cannot fly. However, they are excellent swimmers and they like to eat fish. Arctic foxes are also meat-eaters. They live in the Arctic (North Pole) and have deep, thick fur to keep them warm. The thick fur on their paws allows them to walk on both ice and snow.

1. How are penguins and arctic foxes alike?

   ○ A. They eat plants.

   ○ B. They have thick fur.

   ○ C. They live in extremely cold regions.

2. How are penguins and arctic foxes different?

   ○ A. Penguins eat meat.

   ○ B. Arctic foxes live in cold regions.

   ○ C. Penguins are excellent swimmers.

3. Write another way that penguins and arctic foxes are different.

   _____

   _____

   _____

   _____

   _____

   _____

To parents   Go to page 122 and do Activity 4 with your child.

Extension Activities

Activity 1: The First and the Last Sentence

Skill: Identifying main idea

Choose a short non-fiction text of about 3 to 4 paragraphs. Read the text with your child. Explain to your child that the main idea of a non-fiction text is usually found in the first or last sentence of a paragraph. Read the first paragraph to your child. Underline the sentence that tells you what the main idea of the paragraph is. Then ask your child to read the next paragraph and underline what he thinks is the main idea. Repeat the exercise for the next few paragraphs.

Activity 2: A Picture Tells a Story

Skill: Making Predictions

Use a story your child is unfamiliar with. Show your child the front cover of the book and ask him what he thinks the book is all about based on the picture and the title of the book. Explain that predictions are good guesses based on what we already know. Read the story to your child, pausing at places with information that confirm what he has guessed correctly.

Activity 3: Which Lollipop?

Skill: Identifying fact and opinion

Choose a passage with both facts and opinions. Make 2 lollipop signs; one says "Fact" and the other says "Opinion". Read the passage with your child. Tell your child that a fact is something that is true and an opinion is someone's feelings and thoughts. Real names, times, dates and statistics are clues that the statement is probably a fact. Feeling words are clues that the statement is probably an opinion. Read the passage with your child again, pausing at appropriate places and ask your child to indicate if he thinks it is a fact or opinion by raising the correct lollipop sign. Discuss with your child why he thinks so.

© 2013 Scholastic Education International (S) Pte Ltd   ISBN 978-981-07-3287-5

Activity 4: What's Alike? What's Different?

Skill: Comparing and Contrasting

Choose a fiction book with two main characters. Read the book with your child and get him to highlight information about the two characters in two different colors. Explain to your child that you are going to find ways that the characters are alike and ways that they are different. Record the information gathered using the following Venn diagram.

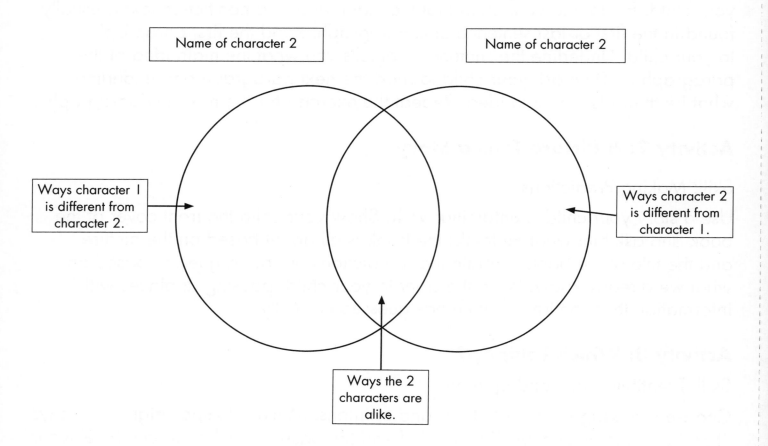

Name of character 2

Name of character 2

Ways character 1 is different from character 2.

Ways character 2 is different from character 1.

Ways the 2 characters are alike.

Answer key

Page 7

1. C   2. C   3. C

Page 8

1. C   2. A   3. C

Page 9

1. B   2. B   3. B

Page 10

1. C   2. A   3. C

Page 11

1. A   2. B   3. C

Page 12

1. B   2. B   3. A

Page 13

1. A   2. A   3. B

Page 14

1. C   2. A   3. C

Page 15

1. C   2. A   3. A

Page 16

1. B   2. C   3. A

Page 17

1. B   2. A   3. B

Page 18

1. B   2. B   3. C

Page 19

1. B   2. A   3. C

Page 20

1. A   2. C   3. C

Page 21

1. A   2. B   3. A

Page 22

1. C   2. B   3. A

Page 23

1. A   2. A   3. C

Page 24

1. B   2. B   3. A

Page 25

1. B   2. A   3. B

Page 26

1. C   2. A   3. A

Page 27

1. A   2. B   3. C

Page 28

1. C   2. A   3. C

Page 29

1. A   2. B   3. A

Page 30

1. C   2. B   3. A

Page 32

1. B   2. A

Page 33

1. B   2. C

© 2013 Scholastic Education International (S) Pte Ltd ISBN 978-981-07-3287-5

Page 34

1. A   2. B

Page 35

1. C   2. C

Page 36

1. A   2. A

Page 37

1. C   2. C

Page 38

1. A   2. B

Page 39

1. C   2. A

Page 40

1. B   2. B

Page 41

1. C   2. B

Page 42

1. B   2. C

Page 43

1. C   2. A

Page 44

1. B   2. B

Page 45

1. A   2. C

Page 46

1. A   2. C

Page 47

1. C   2. B

Page 48

1. B   2. A

Page 49

1. A   2. C

Page 50

1. C   2. B

Page 51

1. C   2. C

Page 52

1. A   2. C

Page 53

1. A   2. A

Page 54

1. C   2. B

Page 55

1. A   2. C

Page 56

1. B   2. B

Page 57

1. A   2. A

Page 58

1. B   2. A

Page 59

1. A   2. B

Page 60

1. A   2. C

Page 62

1. A. opinion   B. fact   C. opinion
2. Teachers can borrow pets for the school months.

Page 63

1. A. fact   B. opinion   C. opinion
2. Possible answers: They don't care to hear someone else's conversation. / People who blab away on mobile phones are really rude.

Page 64

1. A. opinion   B. fact   C. fact
2. Possible answers: Nesting dolls are sets of wooden dolls. / These dolls were first made in Russia in 1890. / They are called Stackable Stars. / Each doll is painted to look like a player on the team.

© 2013 Scholastic Education International (S) Pte Ltd ISBN 978-981-07-3287-5

Page 65

1. A. fact   B. opinion   C. fact
2. In my opinion, you have to be a good sport for this race.

Page 66

1. A. fact   B. opinion   C. opinion
2. They must be rather messy animals.

Page 67

1. A. fact   B. fact   C. opinion
2. Possible answers: The others are lions, tigers and leopards. / A jaguar has a big head and strong jaw. / Its paws and claws are huge. / The jaguar is a silent and deadly hunter. / The jaguar spends most of its time alone and even stays away from other jaguars.

Page 68

1. A. fact   B. opinion   C. fact
2. Vegetable soup seems better to me!

Page 69

1. A. fact   B. opinion   C. fact
2. Possible answers: They spent their free time in other ways. / Sometimes they sailed in boats. / They also picked flowers that grew along the shores.

Page 70

1. A. fact   B. fact   C. opinion
2. This must be the most fun way to play chess.

Page 71

1. A. opinion   B. opinion   C. fact
2. These animals are super.

Page 72

1. A. opinion   B. opinion   C. fact
2. I would not have worked on one of these trains.

Page 73

1. A. fact   B. fact   C. opinion
2. So the owner put a bag over the mirror when the car was parked.

Page 74

1. A. opinion   B. fact   C. fact
2. Gray whales are really amazing.

Page 75

1. A. fact   B. fact   C. opinion
2. Possible answers: When a chick is in its shell, it needs air to breathe. / Then the air passes through a thin skin inside the shell. / At one end of the shell is an air bubble. / When the chick is ready to hatch, it pops this bubble. / Then it practices using its lungs to breathe.

Page 76

1. A. opinion   B. fact   C. opinion
2. Possible answers: I love the idea. / A good slurp and a good burp are fine with me.

Page 77

1. A. opinion   B. fact   C. fact
2. I think this is very exciting.

Page 78

1. A. fact   B. fact   C. opinion
2. Possible answers: People and horses are measured for height in different ways. / It is hard to get a fixed measurement, so horses are measured from their feet to their withers. / The withers are on a horse's back above the shoulders.

Page 79

1. A. fact   B. fact   C. opinion
2. What a great family!

Page 80

1. A. opinion   B. fact   C. fact
2. Eating bread is good for us.

Page 81

1. A. fact   B. opinion   C. fact
2. I think a rainbow has seven colors – red, orange, yellow, green, indigo, blue and violet.

Page 82

1. A. opinion   B. opinion   C. opinion
2. People sometimes keep dogs to guard their houses.

Page 83

1. A. fact   B. opinion   C. fact
2. Possible answers: Over the years, people tamed animals such as oxen, donkeys and horses to help them. / In places where sledges were not suitable, such as on rough ground, men attached sections of logs to heavy objects and rolled them to various places.

Page 84

1. A. fact   B. fact   C. opinion
2. What a comfort!

Page 85

1. A. fact   B. opinion   C. fact
2. Possible answers: Eating mooncakes is one of the popular celebrations of the day. / That was a smart way to communicate.

Page 86

1. A. opinion   B. fact   C. fact
2. A rabbit's home is like a maze.

Page 87

1. A. opinion   B. fact   C. opinion
2. These men do not have any other job except to play football for a team or a club.

Page 88

1. A. fact   B. fact   C. opinion
2. They are the most amazing of all bears.

Page 89

1. A. opinion   B. fact   C. fact
2. In my opinion, this is a practical way to reserve seats.

Page 90

1. A. fact   B. opinion   C. opinion
2. Scientists have been fascinated by the planets in our solar system for many years.

Page 92

1. A   2. B
3. Possible answer: Polly likes to wear T-shirts and pants but the writer likes to wear dresses. / Polly wants to be an astronaut but the writer wants to be an artist.

Page 93

1. A   2. C
3. Possible answer: Both insects and spiders hatch from eggs.

Page 94

1. B   2. B
3. Possible answer: They have learned to do tricks.

Page 95

1. B   2. A
3. Possible answer: Mother turtles cover their eggs and leave.

Page 96

1. A   2. B
3. Possible answer: They are wild cats.

Page 97

1. A   2. A
3. Possible answer: They belong to the same group of insects.

Page 98

1. B   2. C
3. Possible answers: Lake surfers usually go out in winter. / Lake surfers wear long wetsuits to keep warm in the cold waters while ocean surfers usually wear bathing suits and surf in sunny weather.

Page 99

1. A   2. B
3. Possible answer: Formula One cars have specially made bodies and engines while stock cars are regular cars that have been changed for racing.

Page 100

1. B   2. B
3. Possible answer: They are found in different parts of the world.

Page 101

1. C   2. B
3. Possible answers: Jasmine changes the water in her fish tank weekly but Crystal seldom changes the water in her fish tank. / Jasmine feeds her fish once a day but Crystal always forgets to feed her fish.

Page 102

1. C   2. C
3. Possible answers: They have poor eyesight. / They use their sense of smell to find food.

Page 103

1. B   2. A
3. Possible answer: They drop off trees in the fall.

Page 104

1. B   2. B
3. Possible answers: A basketball team has five players, while a baseball team has nine. / The method of scoring is different for baseball and basketball.

© 2013 Scholastic Education International (S) Pte Ltd ISBN 978-981-07-3287-5

Page 105

1. B   2. B

3. Possible answers: They have four legs and no tails. / They use their back legs for jumping.

Page 106

1. A   2. C

3. Possible answers: They help to rescue people. / They usually have loud sirens and flashing lights to alert road users.

Page 107

1. B   2. A

3. Possible answer: A digital camera is for taking photographs.

Page 108

1. A   2. C

3. Possible answer: Astronauts eat foods similar to what we eat on Earth.

Page 109

1. C   2. C

3. Possible answers: They are baleen whales. / They have no teeth. / They have baleen, or thin plates, in their mouth to strain out food.

Page 110

1. B   2. A

3. Possible answers: They are played differently. / The trombone is bigger than the trumpet.

Page 111

1. C   2. A

3. Possible answer: They are popular tales for children.

Page 112

1. B   2. A

3. Possible answers: In the past, only men could compete but now both women and men can participate. / The Olympics were held in Greece in the past, but today, they are held in various cities in the world.

Page 113

1. B   2. B

3. Possible answers: They have scaly skins and lay eggs. / They have long tails, short legs and sharp teeth.

Page 114

1. A   2. B

3. Possible answer: Public transport does not require the users to clean or maintain the vehicle.

Page 115

1. C   2. B

3. Possible answer: They have smooth skin, with almost no hair and are herbivores.

Page 116

1. A   2. C

3. Possible answers: the days are shorter and colder in winter. / It may snow in winter.

Page 117

1. C   2. B

3. Possible answer: They have had their ambitions ever since they attended Career Day.

Page 118

1. B   2. A

3. Possible answers: Huts are temporary shelters. / Huts can be moved easily and can withstand different weather conditions.

Page 119

1. A   2. B

3. Possible answers: They are carnivorous plants. / They eat insects for nutrients.

Page 120

1. C   2. C

3. Possible answers: Penguins live in the Antarctic and arctic foxes live in the Arctic.

© 2013 Scholastic Education International (S) Pte Ltd ISBN 978-981-07-3287-5